The Chickencoop Chinaman

AND

The Year of the Dragon

The Chickencoop Chinaman
AND
The Year of the Dragon

TWO PLAYS
by Frank Chin

INTRODUCTION BY DOROTHY RITSUKO McDONALD

UNIVERSITY OF WASHINGTON PRESS

Seattle and London

Library of Congress Cataloging-in-Publication Data
Chin, Frank, 1940–
    The chickencoop Chinaman.
    Included bibliographical references.
    I. Chin, Frank, 1940–   Year of the dragon.
II. Title.
PS3553.H4897C47   1981   812'.54   81-985
ISBN 0-295-95833-2   AACR2

The Chickencoop Chinaman is dedicated to Elizabeth and Gabriel; Miles and Lowell; Miles, Aaron, and Shokai; Jeremy and Jonathan; Jennifer and Aaron Bear and Godzilla . . . with special thanks to the East-West Players of Los Angeles.

The Year of the Dragon is dedicated to the memory of Louis Chu and John Okada.

Contents

Introduction by Dorothy Ritsuko McDonald   ix

The Chickencoop Chinaman   1

The Year of the Dragon   67

Introduction

1. THE AUTHOR'S SENSE OF HISTORY

"I was born in Berkeley, California in 1940, far from Oakland's Chinatown where my parents lived and worked," begins Frank Chin in his own profile.[1] "I was sent away to the Motherlode country where I was raised through the War. Then back to Chinatowns Oakland and San Francisco. . . . " When offered a fellowship in 1961 for the State University of Iowa's Writer's Workshop, Chin accepted, but soon he was back in the West. "I was the first Chinese-American brakeman on the Southern Pacific Railroad, the first Chinaman to ride the engines. . . . fine riding but I left the rails."

Chinatown, Motherlode country (the Sierra Nevadas), railroads, Chinaman—these are key words for Frank Chin, for they denote his sense of Chinese American history as a valiant, vital part of the history of the American West, a history he believes his own people, under the stress of white racism, have forgotten or wish to forget in their eagerness to be assimilated into the majority culture. But the cost of acceptance has been great, especially for the Chinese male, who finds himself trapped by a stereotype: supposedly lacking in assertiveness, creativity, and aggressiveness, he is characterized as passive, obedient, humble, and effeminate.

For Chin, however, the Chinese men ("Chinamans" as distinguished from assimilated Chinese Americans) who left their families for the New World in the nineteenth century were masculine and heroic, like other "explorers of the unknown—seekers after gold, the big break, the new country. . . ."[2] But the Chinese pioneers

---

1. Frank Chin, "Frank Chin Profile," p. 1.
2. Frank Chin, "Back Talk," *News of the American Place Theatre* 3 (May 1972): 2.

encountered a systematic and violent racism which by now has been well documented.[3] Even Mark Twain, who harbored his own prejudice against the Indians of the West, remarked on the unjust treatment of the Chinese:

> Any white man can swear a Chinaman's life away in the courts, but no Chinaman can testify against a white man. Ours is the "land of the free"—nobody denies that—nobody challenges it. (Maybe it is because we won't let other people testify.) As I write, news comes that in broad daylight in San Francisco, some boys have stoned an inoffensive Chinaman to death and although a large crowd witnessed the shameful deed, no one interfered.[4]

To Chin, Chinatowns were also the products of racism. That the Chinese themselves clustered together to preserve their alien culture is for him a myth: "The railroads created a detention camp and called it 'Chinatown.' The details of that creation have been conveniently forgotten or euphemized into a state of sweet confusion. The men who lived through the creation are dying out, unheard and ignored. When they die, no one will know it was not us that created a game preserve for Chinese and called it 'Chinatown.' "[5]

Given this historical perspective, is it any wonder that echoes of the West would resound in the work of this fifth-generation American, imbued with the aborted dreams of the hardworking, manly goldminers and railroad builders of his past? In Chin's first play, *The Chickencoop Chinaman*, the hero, Tam Lum, tells his children of the pioneers' old American dream:

> Grandmaw heard thunder in the Sierra hundreds of miles away and listened for the Chinaman-known Iron Moonhunter, that train built by Chinamans who knew they'd never be given passes to ride the rails they laid. So of all American railroaders, only they sung no songs, told no jokes, drank no toasts to the ol' iron horse, but stole themselves some iron on the way, slowly stole up a pile of steel, children, and hid there in the granite face of the Sierra and built themselves a wild engine to take

3. See, for instance, Roger Daniels, ed., *Anti-Chinese Violence in North America* (New York: Arno Press, 1979).

4. Mark Twain, *Roughing It* (Berkeley: University of California Press, 1972), p. 350.

5. Frank Chin, "Confessions of the Chinatown Cowboy," *Bulletin of Concerned Asian Scholars* 4 (Fall 1972): 60.

them home. Every night, children, grandmaw listened in the kitchen, waiting, til the day she died."

The Iron Moonhunter, that seeker after the dream, carries the memories and hopes of the proud Chinamen who laid rails across the West.

Chin's grandfather worked as a steward on the Southern Pacific and owned a watch with a train engraved upon it. "I took my grandfather's watch and worked on the Southern Pacific," says Chin. "I rode in the engines up front. . . . I rode in the cabooses where no Chinaman had ever ridden before. I was hired with the first batch of blacks to go braking for the SP, in the 60's when the fair employment legislation went into effect. (Ride with me grandpa, at least it's not the steward service. You get home more often now.)"[6]

In his essay "Confessions of the Chinatown Cowboy," from which the previous quote was taken, Chin describes that rare Western breed, the modern-day Chinaman, in poet and labor-organizer Ben Fee: "a word of mouth legend, a bare knuckled unmasked man, a Chinaman loner out of the old West, a character out of Chinese sword-slingers, a fighter. The kind of Chinaman we've been taught to ignore, and forget if we didn't want America to drive Chinatown out of town."[7]

It was Ben Fee who called Chin the "Chinatown Cowboy" for the dramatic black outfit he wore during their first meeting. "A Chinaman dressed for a barndance," says Chin of his younger self, "solid affectation."[8]

Despite the self-irony displayed here, the black-garbed, two-fang-buckled Chin is obviously no assimilated Chinese; he is declaring his aggressive masculinity and claiming the history of the American West as his own. For the unwary reader, then, who rigidly associates Asian Americans with Asian culture and not American history or culture, some passages in Chin's plays can be disconcerting if not downright incomprehensible or offensive. To such a reader, the meaning of Tam's lyrical monologue on the Iron Moonhunter would

6. Chin, "Confessions," p. 62.
7. Ibid., p. 58.
8. Ibid.

be lost. And what of the Lone Ranger metaphor that dominates the balance of the play? Aware that Asians were excluded from American heroism, Tam Lum during his boyhood had idolized the black-haired Lone Ranger, whose mask, he thought, hid his "slanty" eyes. But in a farcical scene the Ranger is revealed to be a broken-down white racist. A train whistle is heard, and the young Tam recognizes it as that of the Iron Moonhunter. But the Ranger cautions Tam and his friend: "Hear no evil, ya hear me? China boys, you be legendary obeyers of the law, legendary humble, legendary passive. Thank me now and I'll let ya get back to Chinatown preservin your culture!"

Chin's historical perspective is similarly found in his next play, *The Year of the Dragon,* set in San Francisco's Chinatown. The theme of the West is sounded by the family in various ways, especially in the climactic last scene when Pa Eng dies suddenly while struggling with Fred, who later says, "I woulda like to have packed him up into the Sierras and buried him by the railroad . . . I was saving that one for last. . . ."

2. AN ENDANGERED SPECIES

If Chin seeks to preserve the history of the first pioneering Chinamen, he nonetheless looks forward in time and sees—as does Fred Eng in *The Year of the Dragon*—the Chinese Americans as an "endangered species." Not only are the Chinese women like Mattie marrying out white at a rapidly increasing rate, in part no doubt due to the present "sissy" image of the Chinese male, but women have always been outnumbered by men. Historically, the series of discriminatory exclusion laws (1882-1924) made it difficult, then impossible, for both alien and American Chinese to bring their wives from China. Chinatown was therefore essentially a bachelor society. In addition, an American-born woman lost her citizenship when she married a person ineligible for citizenship; and by the Exclusion Act of 1882, immigrant Chinese could not be naturalized. These laws were repealed in 1943 during the Second World War when China was an ally of the United States.[9]

9. Thomas W. Chinn, ed., *A History of the Chinese in California: A Syllabus* (San Francisco: Chinese Historical Society of America, 1969), pp. 26-39. For an extended

In *The Year of the Dragon*, it is mainly through the American-born Ma Eng that the reader discerns this historical discrimination. She tells Ross: "My grandmother, Ross . . . she used to tell me she used to come home oh, crying like a sieve cuz all she saw was blocks and blocks of just men. No girls at all. She was very lonely." Moreover, she says of her daughter: "You know . . . my Sissy is a very limited edition. Only twenty Chinese babies born in San Francisco in 1938." When she discovers that the mysterious visitor in her home is her husband's first wife, who had to be left in China because of the Exclusion Act of 1924 and now could enter America because of its repeal, she says: "I coulda been deported just for marrying your pa. The law scared me to death but it make your pa so thrilling to me. I'm American of Chinese descent. . . ."

However, had Ma Eng, by some stretch of imagination, desired to marry a white American, it would have been illegal at that time, for in California such an intermarriage was forbidden in 1906 by a law which was not nullified until 1948.[10] But at the time of the play not only are the Matties marrying out white, so are the males. Thus, Fred tells Ross, "it's a rule not the exception for us to marry out white. Out in Boston, I might even marry me a blonde." Later, while urging his juvenile-delinquent brother, Johnny, to leave Chinatown for Boston and college, he adds, "Get a white girl while you're young. You'll never regret it."

This urge toward assimilation and extinction is similarly found in *The Chickencoop Chinaman* when Tam Lum, though a loner in the play, is revealed to have been previously married to a white woman who had deserted him, leaving with his two children to take a white husband. During Tam's subsequent effort to restore his dignity, a member of the aging bachelor society advised him about survival in a hostile America: destroy and forget the past; get along with the "Americans."

In an essay entitled "Yellow Seattle," Chin repeats his conviction

study of the bachelor society, see Victor G. and Brett de Bary Nee, *Longtime Californ': A Documentary Study of an American Chinatown* (New York: Pantheon Books/Random House, 1973).

10. H. Mark Lai and Philip P. Choy, *Outlines: History of the Chinese in America* (San Francisco: H. M. Lai & P. P. Choy, 1971), p. 99.

that not only Chinese America but Japanese America is historically doomed, a prediction also made by UCLA sociologist Harry Kitano.[11] "Nationally," says Chin, "between 60 and 70 percent of Japanese Americas are marrying out white. They're abandoning the race, giving up on a people they feel has no history, identity, culture, or art. Chinese Americans aren't far behind. . . . The process of marrying out faster than we can reproduce seems irreversible."[12]

This conviction casts a veil of tragedy over his work, despite its frequently humorous tone. One can see chronologically in his plays an increasing disintegration of both family and self.[13] His heroes, like so many other American heroes, are isolated and wounded. They are articulate but incapable of the action necessary to fulfill the hope and promise of the past.

3. *The Chickencoop Chinaman:*
THE SEARCH FOR THE IDEAL FATHER

Chin is a developing artist, and his first play, which won the East West Players playwriting contest in 1971 and was produced by the American Place Theatre of New York in 1972, is a feast of ideas, a sourcebook of themes and concerns that would be developed in his later work and which, in turn, would influence other Asian American writers. It is a difficult, allusive play. One must be aware of Chin's particular vision of history—his researches into a shrouded past—to understand his elliptical references. Like many other artists, he does not believe that he is constrained to explain his work. Therefore, some readers may be confounded when they do not find here the exotic, standardized comfort, say, of a *Flower Drum Song*.

Critical reaction to the stage production of *The Chickencoop Chinaman* was mixed. Clive Barnes of *The New York Times* (14 June 1972) found it "interesting" because of its ethnic content but did not

11. "Nisei as a group will 'disappear by 2000,' Kitano speculates," *Pacific Citizen*, 25 February 1977, pp. 1-2.
12. Frank Chin, "Yellow Seattle," *The Weekly: Seattle's Newsmagazine*, 1 February 1976, p. 11.
13. *Gee, Pop!*, Chin's unpublished play which has nonetheless been produced, shows the fragmentation of the hero into at least two different characters.

much like the play. Edith Oliver, writing in *The New Yorker*, was delighted by what she saw, describing the play as "theatrical and inventive" and Tam Lum's speeches as a "dazzling eruption of verbal legerdemain" (24 June 1972). Jack Kroll of *Newsweek* found "real vitality, humor and pain on Chin's stage," and said he would "remember Tam Lum long after I've forgotten most of this season's other plays." He thought Chin a "natural writer; his language has the beat and brass, the runs and rim-shots of jazz" (19 June 1972).

Michael Feingold of *The Village Voice* (15 June 1972), who noted that the play was "blossoming all over with good writing, well-caught characters, and sharply noted situations," nevertheless said that when Tam launched into his monologues, "hot air, disguised as Poetry, flies in." Even less complimentary was Julius Novick, also of *The New York Times*, who concluded that while John Osborne was a "master rhetorician," Frank Chin was not.

Given the difficulty of the play, one wonders at the sympathic perception of a Jack Kroll or an Edith Oliver. Betty Lee Sung, author of *Mountain of Gold*, who publicly admits that she and Chin have been "friendly enemies" for years, expressed in *East/West* (3 July 1974) her opinion of *Chickencoop Chinaman:* "I agreed with the drama critics [which ones she does not specify]. I simply did not like the play, nor did the audience, which kept dwindling act after act. My comments: [It]was an outpouring of bitterness and hatred mouthed through lengthy monologue after monologue. Not that it was Randy Kim's fault (the main character actor) but it was Frank Chin showing through." Previously, Chin had publicly declared Sung to be an assimilationist—one who is willing to pay through subservience the "price of acceptance."

In *Chickencoop Chinaman*, Tam Lum epitomizes the cultural and historical dilemma of the incipient Asian American writer. The editors of *Aiiieeeee!* describe him as "the comic embodiment of Asian-American manhood, rooted in neither Asia nor white America" and thus "forced to invent a past, mythology, and traditions from the antiques and curios of his immediate experience."[14]

---

14. Frank Chin et al., eds., *Aiiieeeee!* (Garden City, N. Y.: Anchor Books/ Doubleday, 1975), pp. 34-35.

What is interesting for the American scholar is that Tam's speeches in the first scene deny the stereotype of the Asian American dual personality—he is neither Chinese nor assimilated American, but a new breed of man created by the American experience. Thus he declares to the Dream Girl:

> My dear in the beginning there was the Word! Then there was me! And the Word was CHINAMAN. And there was me. . . . I lived the Word! The Word is my heritage. . . . Born? No! . . . Created! Not born. No more born than heaven and earth. No more born than nylon or acrylic. For I am a Chinaman! A miracle synthetic!

But it is soon apparent that these words are sheer bravado, for even the name of the Dream Girl shows Tam to be enmeshed in history. She is described as a "dream monster from a popular American song of the twenties," a song which parodies the womanless bachelor society.

The ensuing scenes reveal, moreover, that Tam has a deep sense of his own emasculation, his inability to achieve. This is symbolically revealed when the Lone Ranger, whom he had once idolized, unaccountably shoots the innocent youth—the future writer—in the hand. Tam also rejects his own father (whom he nonetheless loves), a dishwasher in a home for the aged, who used to bathe with his shorts on for fear of being peeked at by old white ladies. "Chinamans do make lousy fathers," Tam says later, "I know, I have one." He similarly rejects himself. He had tried to obliterate his Chinese American identity by marrying out white and forgetting the history of his people. And he says of his children: "I don't want 'em to be anything like me or know me, or remember me. This guy they're calling 'daddy' . . . I hear he's even a better writer than me."

For all his self-rejection, however, Tam wishes to discover a more heroic past and identity, and believes his destiny as a writer is "to talk to the Chinaman sons of Chinamans, children of the dead." But the problem of an appropriate language to represent their experience disturbs him. In fact, during the opening scene, the stage directions note that "his own 'normal' speech jumps between black and white rhythms and accents." Ironically Tam says: "I speak nothing but the mother tongues bein' born to none of my own, I talk the talk of orphans." In an interview Chin explains:

Our condition is more delicate than that of the blacks because, unlike the blacks, we have neither an articulated organic sense of our American identity nor the verbal confidence and self-esteem to talk one up from our experience. As a people, we are pre-verbal, pre-literate—afraid of language as the instrument through which the monster takes possession of us. For us American born, both the Asian languages and the English language are foreign. We are a people without a native tongue. To whites, we're all foreigners, still learning English. . . . And to Asians born to Asian culture—Asian by birth and experience and American by choice—our Chinese and Japanese is a fake.[15]

In this context, Tam's self-characterization as a linguistic orphan is made understandable. As the editors of *Aiiieeeee!* point out, "the literary establishment has never considered the fact that a new folk in a strange land would experience the land and develop a new language out of old words."[16]

Conscious of his own emasculation, Tam admires boxers and still hopes he can somehow gain the respect of his children by filming a documentary of the hero of his youth, a black fighter named Ovaltine Jack Dancer, a former light-heavyweight champ. Tam's purpose in flying from California to Pittsburgh is to meet Charley Popcorn, the Dancer's ostensible father, whom the boxer has described in heroic terms. Tam stays at the home of a childhood friend, "Blackjap" Kenji, a research dentist who lives by choice in the black ghetto. Tam enthusiastically looks forward to meeting Charley: "This trip's going to make me well. I'm going to see again, and talk and hear. . . ." Kenji himself is eager: "Father of a champion, man."

Chin's own sympathy for blacks and his acknowledgment of their pioneering efforts in civil rights are revealed in the encounter between the two Asian Americans and Charley, who is puzzled by the appearance of Chinaman Tam after hearing a black voice over the telephone. Charley denies that he is Ovaltine's father and asserts that the Dancer's wonderful tales of an ideal father-son relation are pure fabrications—assertions that the hero- and father-seeking Tam almost hysterically cannot accept. Charley becomes sympathetic, although he confesses that blacks "don't particularly favor Chinese."

15. Chin, "Back Talk," p. 4.
16. Chin et al., eds., *Aiiieeeee!*, p. 22.

He also chastizes Tam for rejecting his own father: "I just know it's wrong to turn your back on your father however old you be."

The next scene finds Tam in "Limbo," symbolically on the black man's back. But later Charley is on Tam's back as Tam staggeringly reenters Kenji's apartment and meets "Tom," an assimilated Chinese who appropriately plays Tonto in the Lone Ranger scene. Tam arouses Kenji's anger by being extremely rude to Tom. Chastized by Kenji, Tam says he will make a straight, professional fight film without a fake father in it, and, accepting his aloneness, retreats to the kitchen to cook dinner for all.

Disappointed in his search for ideality, Tam recalls the family's dream of the Iron Moonhunter:

> Now and then, I feel them old days, children, the way I feel the prowl of the dogs in the night and the bugs in the leaves and the thunder in the Sierra Nevadas however far that are. The way my grandmother had an ear for trains. Listen, children. I gotta go. Ride Buck Buck Bagaw with me . . . Listen in the kitchen for the Chickencoop Chinaman slowin on home.

4. LANGUAGE AS A MEDIUM OF CULTURE

Before we proceed to *The Year of the Dragon*, a brief comment on Chin's use of language may be helpful. Chin confronts the linguistic problem that Tam faces in a bold, revolutionary manner. Some readers may consequently be daunted by his deliberately unconventional style. His language abounds with slang, obscenities, and unusual grammar. The Cantonese terms may also make for difficult reading. But Chin would argue that he has captured the rhythms and accents of Chinese America without which its culture cannot truly be represented. This philosophical position is perhaps most clearly stated in the introduction to *Aiiieeeee!*:

> Language is the medium of culture and the people's sensibility, including the style of manhood. Language coheres the people into a community by organizing and codifying the symbols of the people's common experience. Stunt the tongue and you have lopped off the culture and sensibility. On the simplest level, a man in any culture speaks for himself. Without a language of his own, he no longer is a man. The concept of the dual personality deprives the Chinese-American and Japanese-American of the means to develop their own terms. The tyranny of lan-

guage has been used by white culture to suppress Asian-American culture and exclude it from operating in the mainstream of American consciousness.[17]

So influential have been the editors of *Aiiieeeee!* (Chin, Jeffery Chan, Lawson Inada, and Shawn Wong) in defining the white cultural oppression of Asian American writers that they have, curiously, freed these writers and initiated a literary movement. In fact, the preface and introduction to *Aiiieeeee!* can be likened to Emerson's "American Scholar," written at a critical time in our national history when our fledgling republic, though politically free, struggled under England's cultural dominion. Similarly, *Aiiieeeee!* is a declaration of intellectual and linguisitic independence, and an assertion of Asian American manhood.

Recent Asian American writers' conferences at the Oakland Museum, the University of Washington, and the Mid-Pacific Institute in Hawaii also give testimony that the linguistic experiments urged by the editors are being more widely accepted. For instance, at the 1978 "Talk Story" conference in Hawaii, pidgin English—once thought to be reprehensible and shameful—was considered a valid medium of communication and poetic expression. Indeed, pidgin, a spoken language, was challenging linguists with the problems of codification. *Aiiieeeee!*'s diction and argumentative pattern have further influenced some autobiographical accounts of self-discovery.[18]

Yet the highly-assertive preface and introduction remain controversial, as do the plays of Frank Chin. He has said that he was "chosen to write theater like making war," and this is an apt description.[19] Always in the vanguard, he is an outspoken, articulate, funny writer, unconstrained by literary and stylistic conventions.

5. *The Year of the Dragon:*
The Disintegration of the Chinese American Family

The Year of the Dragon was first produced in 1974 by the Ameri-

17. Ibid., pp. 35-36.
18. See, for instance, Joanne Harumi Sechi, "Being Japanese-American Doesn't Mean 'Made in Japan,' " in *The Third Woman: Minority Women Writers of the United States*, ed. Dexter Fisher (Boston: Houghton Mifflin, 1980), pp. 442-49.
19. Letter to Michael Kirby, ed., *The Drama Review*, 22 Oct.-23 Nov. 1976, pp. 33-34.

can Place Theatre in New York. More traditionally structured than *Chickencoop*, it received generally good notices except from Douglas Watt of *The New York Daily News* (3 June 1974) and Yoshio Kishi of the *New York Nichibei* (6 June 1974), who both found the play incomprehensible. However, a more sympathetic Genny Lim, writing in *East/West* (5 June 1974), found the family drama gripping and the culture and psychological conflicts so realistic that "we are, oftentimes, tempted to watch with our faces averted."

A PBS version for *Theatre in America* was videotaped in 1975. During a 1977 San Francisco production, in which Chin starred, he wrote to a newspaper critic: "The play is set in Frisco, because this city is known as the place our history began. Frisco is the soul of Chinese America. The play is set in the Year of the Dragon because the Dragon was the Bicentennial year. The play sums up where I see Chinese America in the Year of the Dragon: 1976."[20]

To Chin, Chinese America has lost its "soul," or integrity, along with its past. Chinatown is a Shangri-La, a Hollywood set, run by Christian converts. The mission schools first undertook the education of Chinese Americans because of continuing public efforts to segregate or ignore them. The missions nonetheless became political instruments by fostering the ideal of the passive, nonaggressive male who recognizes the superiority of whites, and by eradicating the memory of the bold, pioneering Chinamen of old. The schools also denied other aspects of Chinese American history—the massacres, for instance. Chin observes that "we were indoctrinated into forgetting the names of every burned down or wiped out Chinatown [and became] gah gah for the little town of Bethlehem instead."[21] But despite this indoctrination, Chinese Americans remained tacitly aware of their alien identity. Thus, the Chinatown of *The Year of the Dragon* is not what is seen by the thousands of tourists during the New Year's parade, but the psychological "deathcamp" that is "in the blood of all *juk sing*."[22] In a moment of compounding frustrations, the hero, Fred Eng, cries out: "I am shit. This family is shit.

20. Letter to Bernard Weiner, 12-13 April 1977, p. 2.
21. Letter to Michael Kirby, p. 15.
22. Chin, "Confessions," p. 65.

Chinatown's shit. You can't love each other around here without hating yourself."

The play, with its theme of disintegration, begins with the imminent death of the father. Having lived in America since 1935, he is now the respected "Mayor" of Chinatown, probably by virtue of his presidency of the Christian-dominated Chinese Benevolent Society. Realizing death is near, he is anxious about the future of his family outside Chinatown's confines, because of his dislike and suspicion of whites. Though at times brutally autocratic and selfish, he is loved by his children and wife; and the family thus has a semblance of unity.

He married Ma Eng when she was but fifteen. Through her carefully recited clichés, she shows that she has been mission-educated: "I always told you to be proud to be the best of the East, the best of the West." "Miss Thompson, she said, 'Talking two completely incompatible languages is a great asset.'" Unconsciously, Ma Eng sings repeatedly the American-written *Chinese Lullabye*, which tells of the selling of "slave girls" (purportedly saved by the missions). She loves her home and family, and fears change. She is nonetheless aware of the slow disintegretion of her family (her husband is dying; her forty-year-old, still unmarried son, Fred, rarely sleeps at home; Johnny is on probation for carrying a gun; Mattie has married out white and has only returned to Chinatown at her father's request); and she attempts to escape moments of stress by going to the bathroom or bursting into song. But she spiritedly objects to the unexpected appearance of Pa Eng's first wife, brought over from China so that he would be surrounded by "happy families when I die. . . ." Nevertheless, in the uproar that follows, she accepts China Mama's presence to preserve as best she can the family integrity. She even adheres to Pa's request that she instruct China Mama in some English by teaching her the *Chinese Lullabye*.

Unlike her mother, Mattie has escaped entirely. She hates Chinatown and asserts that her home is now in Boston with her white husband, Ross. Years ago, she made clear her intention to leave forever, noting that "it didn't matter where I was born or what color I was . . . especially being a Chinese girl." She was obviously aware of her desirability to white men.

Her brother Johnny brings forth the undercurrent of violence in Chinatown which destroys the image of the strong, law-abiding Chinese American family. Before his appearance, we are informed that his friend has been shot and killed that day. Vigorously hostile to Ross, Johnny is an alienated youth, preferring his criminal escapades with immigrant hoodlums—whose language he cannot understand—to college and Boston and the world his sister has chosen. When Mattie urges that they all leave for Boston after Pa Eng's death ("Out there we'll be able to forget we're Chinamen, just forget all this and just be people . . ."), Johnny replies coldly, "You have to forget you're a Chinatown girl to be just people, sis?"

His older brother, Fred, the head of Eng's Chinatown Tour 'n Travel, hates Chinatown for being the whites' "private preserve for an endangered species." But as Chinatown's top guide with an inimitable spiel, Fred hates himself even more. He knows that he has lost sight of his dream of being a writer and, moreover, his job forces him to conform to the American stereotype of Chinese Americans. According to Chin, a tourist guide is by definition "a Chinaman, playing a white man playing Chinese. . . . A minstrel show. The tourist guides of Chinatown are traditionally the despised and perverted."[23]

Thus Fred's spiels to the tourists are given in a language and manner expected by them. The model on which these expectations are based is Charlie Chan, a character invented by a white man in 1925 and invariably played by white men in the movies and on television. Though intelligent, Chan has the expected Asian American qualities: he is humble, passive, polite, self-effacing, and effeminate, and has difficulties with English.[24] Ross, Mattie's white husband, shows

23. Letter to Bernard Weiner, p. 2.
24. In his 1971 interview with Roland Winters, the last of the movie Charlie Chans, Chin asked why NBC chose Ross Martin, a white, to play the television detective. Winters replied: "I don't know. The only thing I can think of, if you uh. If you want to cast a homosexual in a show, and you get a homosexual, it'll be awful. It won't be funny. If you get a normal man, playing a homosexual it's funny. And maybe there's something there." Confucianisms were also a source of humor, as was Chan's habit of referring to himself in the third person. Chin also noted the slight accent that Winters used in the role. Winters replied that it was "more of an accent than that really. *And a slightly higher voice*" [italics mine]. Winters went on to say that the educated Orientals he had known were well-mannered, "very simple, and very

his acceptance of the Chan sterotype by reciting Confucianisms and suggesting that Pa Eng, as Mayor of Chinatown, add a Charlie Chan joke to his speech to be given after the parade. Therefore, before Pa leaves for the occasion, he greets Fred with "You got dah case solve yet?" and insists that Fred, his "Number One Son," call him "Pop": "Gosh, Pop!" "Gee, Pop!"

Fred's own perception of Chan is found earlier in a scene with China Mama, his real mother recently from China. He responds to her question, given, of course, in Chinese:

> You want me to be Chinese too, huh? Everybody does . . . You know how the tourists tell I'm Chinese? No first person pronouns. No "I," "Me" or "We." I talk like that lovable sissy, Charlie Chan, no first person personal pronouns, and instant Chinese culture . . . ha, ha, ha. . . .

Continuing to speak to her uncomprehending ears, Fred declares himself to be a Chinaman:

> I'm not Chinese. This ain't China. Your language is foreign and ugly to me so how come you're my mother? . . . I mean, I don't think I'm quite your idea of a son, either . . . You hear all my first person pronouns, China Mama. . . . Just because we're born here don't mean we're nobody and gotta go away to another language to talk. I think Chinatown Buck Buck Bagaw is beautiful.

The use of the first person pronouns is for Fred the declaration of his American individualism and individual rights. He had wanted to become a writer and be "something special," not just his father's son. But having been born in China and having entered America illegally as an infant, he is torn between his desire for his own life and his responsibilities to his family. The mixture of the old and the new may be seen in some of Fred's small gestures. Twice he lights incense for the ancestral shrine before lighting up a "joint." More importantly, ten years earlier, while yet in college pursuing his

---

courteous." They did a lot of bowing instead of responding verbally, and kept their hands to their sides. Although Winters thought of Chan as being physically courageous, the directors did not want him to do "any physical stuff." [Frank Chin, "Interview: Roland Winters," *Amerasia Journal* 2 (Fall 1973): 1-19.] Chin adds in the preface, "In the days when Charlie Chan was a bit part two Japanese actors Shojnin and George Kuwa briefly were thrown to light on the screen."

dream of being a writer, he was called home by his father, who was dying from a lung complaint. As the eldest son, Fred was expected to be obedient, to earn money for the family, and to be responsible for his younger siblings. In fact, Fred is chastized by his father for Johnny's delinquency, and Sis recalls that in the past it was Fred who was beaten for her misbehavior.

Despite his hatred for his job, Fred is proud of his successful shouldering of family responsibilities. He has enabled Mattie to go away to college and, upon her arrival, gives her the traditional New Year's monetary envelope to present to Pa Eng. He talks of Boston, where her Mama Fu Fu business is prospering, as a place for the revivification of the family. Almost nightly he attends his sick father in the bathroom. But for all his fidelity and success, Fred expects some gratitude and respect from his father. Consequently he is enraged when Pa imports China Mama without consulting him and when Pa declares him to be a "flop," unable to care for the family outside Chinatown's confines.

But Pa, for all his Chinese roots, has taken on the values of this American Chinatown. Though demanding unquestioning obedience from Fred, he ironically selected a tourist guide business for him, a business despised by Chinatown. Thereafter, Pa has never acknowledged his children in print, and once, while lunching with Fred, he did not even bother to introduce his son when other Chinatown dignitaries approached. Although it was Pa who removed Fred from college, he disdains Fred's ambition to be a writer, valuing only the more lucrative and traditional professions—which require a college degree. In preparing his New Year's speech, Pa hurts Fred by asking Ross, a "real" American, for help; but in his own insecurity with English he asks Fred privately to edit the first draft so that Ross will not discover his ineptness.

Since China Mama was brought to America so that Pa could die "Chinese," Fred asks him why he did not return to China instead. Pa replies that he regards Chinatown in America as his home. This for Chin is significant, as he believes most Chinese came here not as sojourners who would eventually return to China but as immigrants, like their European counterparts, with their own vision of America.

Pa, in this bathroom scene, is aware that the family line has probably come to an end and attempts to exact from Fred a promise that he will always remain in Chinatown. Of Mattie, Pa says: "Sissy go colleges and what happening? Bok gwai low! [White devil!] And no more blood. No more Chinese babies born in family. No Merican Chinese babies, nutting doing and flop." Fred is forty, balding, single, and unlikely to marry. Johnny's criminal escapades will probably kill him eventually.

During the last scene of the play, as the festive sounds of the parade float into the room, Fred asks his father to look at him for once as an individual and not just as a son. Aware of his father's power over Ma and Johnny, who are rapidly deteriorating, Fred promises to remain in Chinatown if Pa will tell Ma and Johnny to leave for Boston. But Pa refuses adamantly, and dies during their physical struggle. At the beginning of his aborted speech, Pa was to have introduced Fred as his heir: "dah one who're teck obber solve dah case. My's Number One Son, allaw time, saying 'Gee, Pop!' Fred Eng!"

At first fearing to leave Chinatown to become a "nobody" or discover that his writing ability has died, Fred is further crippled by his father's inability to the very end to see him as an individual. As the lights fade before his final spiel, Fred—his father's heir—is "dressed in solid white, puts on a white slightly oversized jacket, and appears to be a shrunken Charlie Chan, an image of death. He becomes the tourist guide."

6. KWAN KUNG: THE IDEAL DISCOVERED

The masculine ideal that Tam Lum sought and the bold individualism that Fred Eng desired, Chin would eventually find in Kwan Kung, a popular folk hero revered throughout the centuries as a god who had, according to Henri Doré, S. J., "fought many battles, was brave, generous, loyal to the Han dynasty. . . . He was a powerful giant, nine feet tall according to one legend, with a beard two feet long. His features 'were of a swarthy colour, and his lips of a bright rosy hue. His eyebrows resembling those of the phoenix. His whole appearance inspired a feeling of terror.' " Kwan is said to have told

his new friend, Liu-pei, that he had wandered over the country for
five years as a fugitive from justice and a champion of the oppressed,
"for I have killed a prominent man, who oppressed the people of my
native place. I have heard that men are being recruited to repress
brigandage, and I wish to join the expedition."[25]

Because of his skill in battle, Kwan came to be deified as the god
of war, and his virtues inspired writers and scholars, whom he pro-
tected. Characteristically, statues of Kwan show him in both a
scholar's robes and a general's uniform. Chin, naturally enough,
interrelates these two aspects. In a letter to Michael Kirby, editor of
The Drama Review, he says that Kwan was "the god of war to soldiers, the god of plunder to soldiers and other arrogant takers, the
god of literature to fighters who soldier with words, and the god
patron protector of actors and anyone who plays him on stage."[26]

Though revered by the Cantonese—who became the first "Chinamans"—the red-faced Kwan was never as "heavy" as the Christian God, according to Chin. Besides being militant, loyal, and
vengeful, Kwan was also selfish and individualistic. This, in Chin's
eyes, restored the image of the integrated self that he saw historically disintegrating: "The Chinese used to say the Cantonese were
so individualistic, they didn't get along with or trust anyone, not
even each other. You could never get close to a Cantonese cuz he
either told you everything endlessly and entertainingly and you
couldn't sort our what counts—or he told you nothing. EVERY CAN-
TONESE IS WHOLE UNTO HIMSELF AS A PLANET and trusts no other
living thing."[27]

Kwan Kung traveled to America with the Cantonese immigrants
through the national epic *The Romance of the Three Kingdoms* in
the forms of both novel and opera. Sprawling and complex in struc-
ture, the *Romance* even in its condensed version reads like Malory's
Works. The most popular of Cantonese operas, for Chin it seems "a
collection of documents, various story tellers' cheat sheets, doggerel

25. Henri Doré, S. J., *Researches into Chinese Superstitions*, trans. M. Kennelly
(Shanghai: T'usewei Press, 1920) 6: 73.
26. Letter to Michael Kirby, p. 2.
27. Ibid., p. 3.

and repeats of folk hearsay by different people writing at different times about the same historical event." It disdains the Western neoclassical unities and is the result "of thousands of years of literate storytelling wordhappy culture." More importantly, both novel and opera "pose as raw documentary history. The form contains the notion of destroying a people by destroying their history. . . ."[28]

The opera also contains the famed fraternal Oath in the Peach Garden sworn by the three heroes: Liu-pei, Kwan Kung, and Chang-fei. They declare their "everlasting friendship" and pledge mutual assistance in all dangers.[29] "It's a soldier's blood oath of loyalty and revenge," says Chin:

> Nothing charitable, necessarily honorable, in any Western sense, passive or timid about it. . . . It encouraged an aggressive self-reliance and trust nobody, watch out killer's sense of individuality that reached a peak in China with the Cantonese, took to the image of what the Chinamans scratching out mountains for gold thought of themselves, grew roots in California and sprouted a Kwan Kung happy race of people who wanted to hear, read, and rewrite, only one story, and sing and sit through and pass with one opera only.[30]

But, says Chin, the imported Cantonese opera became "purely Chinaman" in expression "as it adjusted language, style, detail, event, and setting to the changing world of the Chinamans at work on a new experience, making new language to define the experience, and make new history." Such were the changes made that for "Chinamans in mining and railroad camps and Chinatown," the opera became "a one man medicine show done by traveling kung fu fighters selling their personal kung fu brew. . . ." Whole families of such fighters "traveled by wagon from camp to camp selling tonic, breaking chains, and doing flash versions of *Three Kingdoms*."[31]

It is to this Chinaman version of Cantonese opera that Chin owes his artistic origins: "I write from links with the original whoremothers of our people and through my mother, ties to the most popular

28. Ibid., p. 5a.
29. Doré, *Researches,* pp. 74-75.
30. Letter to Michael Kirby, p. 11.
31. Ibid.

hero of the most popular novel and opera living with me. The Kwan
blood from my mother meant I was chosen to write theater like
making war, throw everything away and get even."[32]

Chin therefore says: "I am not any white writer. I'm Frank Chin,
Chinaman writer. White reviewers like Julius Novick and Clive
Barnes stuck in their Christian esthetic of one god, one good, one
voice, one thing happening, one talk at a time get so dizzy in the
atmosphere of Chinaman word strategy they gotta cancel out every
white writer they know to make sense of my simple Chinaman back-
scratch."[33] He believes that an artist should be judged on his own
terms, and that to apply the traditional Western criteria to his work
is irrelevant and unfair.

Yet, in his conception of a New Man (a Chinaman) and a new language wrought out of the new American experience, Chin shows his
awareness of the early nineteenth-century American struggle for
cultural and linguistic freedom from Britain. Moreover, to counter
the effeminate, Christianized Charlie Chan image of the post-1925
era, he has restored the immensely masculine Kwan Kung, whose
strength of mind and body, individuality and loyalty, capacity for
revenge, and essential aloneness are reminiscent of the rugged
Western hero of American myth. The interested reader might wish
to contrast this rugged individualism with the perception of Chinese
character in Francis L. K. Hsu's *The Challenge of the American
Dream: The Chinese in the United States*.[34] Professor Hsu is an immigrant Chinese.

Kwan Kung's opera also contains an idea that haunts Chin's work:
the destruction of a people by destroying their history. Chin is well
aware of white fears in this vein; one of his more amusing insights is
of James Hilton's Shangri-La as a place designed for the preserva-
tion of white culture, where whites with low self-esteem can be wor-
shipped and serviced by yellows. He is regretful, on the other hand,
that his own generation has forgotten their past and their old hero:

32. Ibid., pp. 33-34.
33. Ibid., p. 8.
34. Francis L. K. Hsu, *The Challenge of the American Dream: The Chinese in the United States* (Belmont, Ca.: Wadsworth Publishing Co., 1971).

"There was a statue of Kwan Kung in every Chinese American home I was ever in," he says, "til my generation moved into houses of their own, and hadn't known 'Chinaman' is what we called ourselves in the English we spoke and made our own for three generations now."[35]

Though acknowledging the eventual extinction of Asian America, Chin in his own life and work has maintained the heroic stance of the old Chinaman god. Recently in a restaurant in Seattle, Chin (who avows he dislikes broken men) was revolted by an aging, embittered No-No Boy of the Second World War who felt his life had been ruined by his imprisonment. "He'd lost all sense of Seattle as a Japanese-American city, all sense of vision," said Chin:

> "You say the Chinese came here with a vision too?" he whined, and I had to move or melt into a pool of boo-hoo and booze and give up with the old man.

> "Get up! Come with me right now!" I said and was walking to the front of the restaurant.

> If he had caught up with me, I'd have collared him and dragged him to the poster of Kwan Kung sitting on his tiger throne with his squire at his right hand, holding Kwan's seal. Kwan's left side robed him like a scholar and his right side armored him like a soldier. "That's the vision of ourselves when we first came over," I said.[36]

35. Letter to Michael Kirby, p. 11.
36. Chin, "Yellow Seattle," p. 11.

The Chickencoop Chinaman

The Chickencoop Chinaman was first produced at the American Place Theatre, New York City, 27 May 1972:

Directed by Jack Gelber
Scenery by John Wulp
Costumes by Willa Kim
Lighting by Roger Morgan

Cast (in order of appearance)

TAM LUM	Randall "Duk" Kim
HONG KONG DREAM GIRL	Joanna Pang
KENJI	Sab Shimono
LEE	Sally Kirkland
ROBBIE	Anthony Marciona
THE LONE RANGER	Merwin Goldsmith
TONTO	Calvin Jung
CHARLEY POPCORN	Leonard Jackson
TOM	Calvin Jung

Characters

TAM LUM, *a Chinese American writer filmmaker with a gift of gab and an open mouth. A multi-tongued word magician losing his way to the spell who trips to Pittsburgh to conjure with his childhood friend and research a figure in his documentary movie.*

HONG KONG DREAM GIRL, *a dream monster from a popular American song of the twenties.*

KENJI, *a research dentist. Japanese American born and raised. Tam's childhood friend. Sullen, brooding. A zombie with taps on his shoes.*

LEE, *possible Eurasian or Chinese American passing for white. She's borne several kids in several racial combinations, but mothers only one, Robbie, her weird son.*

ROBBIE, *Lee's weird son.*

THE LONE RANGER, *a legendary white racist with the funk of the West smouldering in his blood. In his senility, he still loves racistly, blesses racistly, shoots straight and is cuckoo with the notion that white folks are not white folks but just plain folks.*

TONTO, *a decrepit faithful Indian companion who's gone out of style.*

CHARLEY POPCORN, *an ancient former boxing trainer and entrepreneur who runs a pornie movie house in Pittsburgh. Tam Lum has come to visit him.*

TOM, *a Chinese American writer. One of Lee's former husbands.*

Place

The Oakland district of Pittsburgh, Pa.

Time

The late sixties.

Settings

ACT ONE   SCENE 1: Tam's Hong Kong Dream Girl dream: scream-
                   ing into Pittsburgh.
          SCENE 2: Kenji's apartment. Early evening.

ACT TWO   SCENE 1: Tam's dream Lone Ranger: the legendary
                   radio childhood.
          SCENE 2: Charley Popcorn's pornie house. Pittsburgh,
                   night.
          SCENE 3: Tam in Limbo.
          SCENE 4: Kenji's apartment. Later that night.

ACT ONE

Scene One

Curtain rises to Limbo stage. Black.

The sound of a screaming jet in flight runs for several seconds. In the dark a chuckle is heard, a mischievous but not sinister little laugh from TAM LUM. *Overriding his chuckle, the voice of* HONG KONG DREAM GIRL *as the stewardess and in-flight presence.*

HONG KONG DREAM GIRL (*as stewardess, voice-over in Limbo*): Ladies and Gentlemen, we are preparing to land in Pittsburgh. Please see that your seatbelts are securely fastened and your seat backs in the upright raised position and observe the no smoking sign. For your comfort and safety we ask that you remain seated and keep your seatbelts fastened until the plane has come to a complete stop. Thank you.

(*Overhead spot comes on. Upstage and high on a platform,* TAM *stands in a shaft of light. The rest of the stage is dark.*)

TAM: She asked me if I thought she looked like she was born in Hong Kong. She looked all right to me except that I thought she was maybe fresh in from drill team practice.

(*Enter* GIRL *dressed as* TAM *describes. She struts and turns across the stage to the rhythm of brush and drums, from one pool of light to the next. She is Asian, beautiful, grinning, doll-like, and mechanical. A wind-up dream girl steppin' out.*)

TAM: . . . because she was wearing high white boots with tassels and a satin dress that had no epaulets on it. And underneath one of them super no-knock, rust-proof, titstiffening bras, with the seams and rivets and buckles showing through. And she walked like she was on parade. And had a drill team Jackie Kennedy,

5

nondescript bouffant hairdo. And hands! Hands just made to hold, not to speak of twirl a baton. Yessir, hands like greased smoothbore cannons. So she asked if I thought she looked like she was born in Hong Kong.

GIRL: Do you think I look like I was born in Hong Kong?

TAM: "Sure you do, Honey," I said, thinking back to the days of high school assemblies and the girl with medals jingling on her satin and sequin chest. Twirling her baton! I especially remember her flaming baton number done in black light to the Ritual Fire Dance. She said, "You. . ."

GIRL: You can tell I was born in Hong Kong, even though I've been here six years?

TAM: . . . She asked. And I replied, "And there's a whole lot more where that came from!"

GIRL: Where were you born?

TAM: Chinamen are made, not born, my dear. Out of junk-imports, lies, railroad scrap iron, dirty jokes, broken bottles, cigar smoke, Cosquilla Indian blood, wino spit, and lots of milk of amnesia.

GIRL: You sure have a way with the word, but I wish you'd do more than pay lip service to your Canton heritage.

(*Through the rest of the speech in this segment,* TAM *goes through voice and accent changes. From W. C. Fields to American Midwest, Bible Belt holy roller, etc. His own "normal" speech jumps between black and white rhythms and accents.*)

TAM: My dear in the beginning there was the Word! Then there was me! And the Word was CHINAMAN. And there was me. I lipped the word as if it had little lips of its own. "Chinaman" said on a little kiss. I lived the Word! The Word is my heritage. Ah, but, it has been many a teacake moon, many thousands of pardons for a dirty picture snapped in my raw youth now, that these lips have had a hankering for servicing some of my Canton heritage in the flesh. But I've never been able to get close enough. Now you, my Hong Kong flower, my sweet sloe-eyed beauty from the mysterious East, I can tell that your little fingers have twiddled many a chopstick. Your smoothbore hands have the memory of gunpowder's invention in them and know how to shape a blast and I dare say, tickle out a shot. Let me lead your hands.

GIRL: I can tell you are really Longtime Californ', and kind of slick too, but you were telling me of what you were made.

TAM: I am the natural born ragmouth speaking the motherless bloody tongue. No real language of my own to make sense with, so out comes everybody else's trash that don't conceive. But the sound truth is that I AM THE NOTORIOUS ONE AND ONLY CHICKEN-COOP CHINAMAN HIMSELF that talks in the dark heavy Midnight, the secret Chinatown Buck Buck Bagaw. I am the result of a pile of pork chop suey thrown up into the chickencoop in the dead of night and the riot of dark birds, night cocks and insomniac nympho hens running after strange food that followed. There was Mother Red built like a fighting cock and running like one too. Hellbent for feather, cocksure, running for pork chop suey in the dead of night. And DESTINY.

GIRL: And then you were born?

TAM: No, lass. Moonlight shone through the chinks of the coop. And seabreezes from the West brought the smell of the ships and the sewers. Moonlight caught prickly in her mad hen's eye and seabreeze in her feathers as she ran a dumb cluck in a bird gallop across the great dung prairie of an Oakland Chinatown Chickencoop. Following Mother Red was her Rhode Island featherbrains. Nickel and dime birds that even after being flat on their backs in Freudian analysis couldn't grunt out an egg between them. Promiscuous and criminal birds. Too lazy even to shape up a proper pecking order, they just grooved on running their fool heads off together, making chicken poetry after Mad Mother Red.

GIRL: And then you were born?

TAM: Meanwhile, back at the doghouse was a bird of a different feather. A mean critter with Red in its eyes, seen as it heard them clucks come loco around the corner.

GIRL: And then you were born?

TAM: No. Just at this moment coming through the fence was a troupe of Spanish Flamenco gypsy dwarves, Los Gitanos Cortos, taking a shortcut to their boxcar after a hard night's work dancing on the tops of Cadillacs and Lincolns in the T&D theatre parking lot. This crowd of shortstuff whiffed the pork chop and had visions of licking their trough clean. Like the mad dog, they ran full of wild Injuns. Blood whooping fast for to grab a quick bite.

GIRL: And then you were born?

TAM (*as a Bible Belt preacher*): Born? No! Crashed! Not born. Stamped! Not born! Created! Not born. No more born than the heaven and earth. No more born than nylon or acrylic. For I am a Chinaman! A miracle synthetic! Drip dry and machine washable. For now, in one point of time and space, as never before and never after, in this one instant of eternity, was focused that terrific, that awesome power of the universe that marks a moment divine . . . For Mother Red and her herd of headless wonders! One mad hairy dog! And twelve little people in high heeled shoes, once and for all, blind and deaf and very dumb to the perpetration of righteous heinous love MET!

GIRL: And then you were born?

   (TAM *gives razzberry.*)

GIRL: And you were born.

TAM: Born. Born to talk to Chinaman sons of Chinamans, children of the dead. But enough of my sordid past. It's not right for a body to know his own origins, for it leaves the mother nothing secret to herself. I want to hear about you.

GIRL: You sure have a way with words, but I'd like it better if you'd speak the mother tongue.

TAM: I speak nothing but the mother tongues bein' born to none of my own, I talk the talk of orphans. But I got a tongue for you, baby. And maybe you could handmake my bone China.

   (TAM *and* GIRL *are in a single pool of light.* TAM *moves to put her hand on his fly and stuff one of his hands inside her shirt.* TAM *licks his lips and puckers up for a smooch, breathing heavy. She giggles and runs off. Blackout.*)

   GIRL (*as stewardess, voice-over in black*): Ladies and Gentlemen, we have just landed in Pittsburgh. The time is now five forty-six, Eastern Standard Time. The temperature is 44 degrees. The weather is cloudy with a chance of snow.

   [Curtain]

SCENE TWO

KENJI's *apartment. Night.*

Pittsburgh's black ghetto is called "Oakland." It has the look of having been a high class, fashionable residential district at the turn of the century. The buildings are still solid, thick-walled . . . at least they seem that way on the outside. Inside the grand interiors have been lost after countless remodelings.

KENJI's *apartment is highceilinged. New diaphragm walls divide what was once a big room into three. The bathroom, complete with tub and sink, the living-dining room and entry area, and part of the kitchen are visible.*

The apartment has the look of having been recently moved into, while at the same time looking a long time settled. It is on the verge of having a style. A massive round table top is set low on the floor on cinder blocks. Wooden auditorium chairs. An over-stuffed chair. A mattress and boxspring from a double bed serves as a couch. Tatami on the floor.

The walls are covered with posters of black country, blues and jazz musicians that clash with the few Japanese prints and art objects.

A cake with one piece cut from it is on the table. Sewing paraphernalia and curtain material are on the table.

The front door is open. Snow is seen falling outside through a window. The crash of cars coupling up from the railyard can be heard now and then.

TAM *and* KENJI *enter.* TAM *carries a small suitcase and an attaché case.* KENJI *carries a travelbag of suits.* TAM *puts his stuff down in the entryway.* KENJI *keeps the travelbag.* TAM *flexes, shakes his legs down, stretches and yawns, scanning the place . . .*

KENJI: Well, man, this is it. My place . . . right in the heart of the black ghetto. Just like home.

TAM: BlackJap Kenji! Mah brother! Whew, man, I thought for awhile you'd grown up, man. Twenty grand high class research dentist wit' his own lab, man, his own imported apes, twenty-three hunnerd miles from the childhood. Grownup, fat, middle-class! Ha. But here ya are, still livin in a slum, still my blackJap Kenji.

KENJI: Who you callin "grownup?"

TAM (*spying curtain stuff*): Yeah, Kenji's home in this Pittsburgh, with a woman and everything. Janet?

KENJI: Naw man, that was . . . where was that?

TAM: High school. I was going to ask you . . .

KENJI: You okay?

TAM: . . . Must be me. Them hours winging here sittin on my ass broke my momentum. I feel like I lost speed . . . It's even hard for me to talk . . . and if I can't talk to you, you know I . . . and I been doing a lotta talkin, Yeah . . . Mumbo Jumbo. Dancer sends his love.

TAM *flops in whatever's handy, leans back and closes his eyes . . .* KENJI *watches him.*

LEE (*sleepily from bedroom*): Robbie? Kenji?

(KENJI *responds to the voice by going to the bedroom and peeking in. He makes a quick survey of the apartment, looking into rooms, seeing who's where. He creeps up on* TAM, *brings his face down close and level with* TAM's *face and turns on Helen Keller . . .*)

KENJI (*as Helen Keller*): Moowahjeerfffurher roar rungs!

(TAM *snaps awake, staring* KENJI *in the face, and deadpan says . . .*)

TAM (*as Helen Keller*): Moowahjeerffurher roar rungs?

KENJI (*as Helen Keller*): Moowahjeerfurher roar rungs.

TAM *and* KENJI (*continuing*): My dear friends!

TAM (*continuing*): Helen Keller! I'd know that voice anywhere!

(TAM *and* KENJI *exchange five.*)

KENJI (*as Helen Keller*): Aheeeha op eeehoooh too ooh wahyou oooh.

TAM (*as a Bible Belt preacher*): Yeah, talk to me, Helen! Hallelujah! I hear her talkin to me.

(TAM *jumps to his feet shuddering with fake religious fervor.* KENJI *supports with Hallelujahs and repetitions.*)

TAM: Put your hands on the radio, children, feel the power of Helen Keller, children. Believe! And she, the Great White goddess, the mother of Charlie Chan, the Mumbler, the Squeaker, shall show you the way, children! Oh, yeah!

KENJI: Hallelujah!

TAM: Helen Keller overcame her handicaps without riot! She overcame her handicaps without looting! She overcame her handicaps without violence! And you Chinks and Japs can too. Oooh I feel the power, children. Feel so gooooood! I feeeeeel it!

(*Enter* ROBBIE *from the kitchen. He wears a bibbed apron. A professional apron, white, no frills.*)

LEE: Tom? Tom? Kenji?

TAM: (*as Helen Keller*): Yarr roar heh yelp wee ooh sub coawt unh ree-ssurch llee-dung toth enged roh dove fub earthed eff fecks.

KENJI (*as Helen Keller*): Your help will support research leading to the end of birth defects . . .

TAM: Listen to the voice of the Great White Motha, come to show you the light, Chinks and Japs, I say Listen, Children! Whooo I feel the power!

(TAM *and* KENJI *exchange fives.* ROBBIE *is attracted to the action, comes and stands, makes himself available, grinning, looking from face to face, laughing.*)

TAM (*as Helen Keller*): nggg gah gallop nose weather bar hearth death facts sorrel lull heed new worm who whirl eye fees.

KENJI: And help those born with birth defects lead normal lives.

TAM: Believe!

KENJI: I believe!

TAM: I said, believe children!

KENJI *and* ROBBIE: I believe!

TAM: AH MEAN! BELIEVE!

KENJI *and* ROBBIE: I believe!

TAM: Hallelujah!

(TAM *and* KENJI *exchange five.* TAM *notices* ROBBIE, *glances at* KENJI, *grins, takes* ROBBIE's *hand, and sets it to give him five, and gives him five.* LEE *rushes angrily into the scene, too late to stop* ROBBIE *from returning five, and grabs her son.*)

LEE: Kenji!

TAM: Sister! Child!

KENJI: For the sake of tomorrow's children.

TAM *and* KENJI (*as Helen Keller*): Thak ahhhnggkkk are are arf rung youuuu.

KENJI: Thank you.

> (TAM *and* KENJI *strut and exchange five, laughing and sparring.*)

KENJI: Remember Helen Keller's telephone?

TAM: It doesn't ring . . .

KENJI: It just gets warm!

> (TAM *less energetically, suddenly preoccupied, goes through the motions of exchanging five with* KENJI, *who wants to snuffle and spar.* ROBBIE *gets his five from* TAM *and stuffs himself into the scene sparring with* KENJI *while* TAM *catches his breath, and rubs his face.*)

LEE (*to* TAM): Leave my boy alone!

TAM: Wha . . . ? What's happening? I got nothing but out-takes in my head . . .

LEE (*to* KENJI): I'm tired of you coming in like this! I'm tired of you putting my son down! Go get your nuts off beating up your own kid! Go on! Come here, Robbie.

ROBBIE: I'm okay Lee.

TAM: How many kids you got?

LEE: . . . What's it to you?

KENJI: None.

TAM (*as Helen Keller*): Oh. Oh . . .

LEE: Oh, you . . . Think you're funny?

KENJI: Everything's cool.

LEE: I've never seen anything so . . .

KENJI: I said, everything's cool!

LEE: You never shout at me. Why're you shouting?

KENJI: Lee . . . Lee, this is my friend, Tam Lum. We used to call him "Tampax" . . .

LEE: Oh, lovely.

KENJI: . . . a long time ago. What's wrong?

LEE: I guess Kenji's told you about me. He tells all his friends.

TAM: No.

KENJI: Friends?

LEE: . . . that I'm pregnant and on my way to Africa.

TAM: No.

KENJI: How can you be pregnant? Who? What?

LEE: . . . and of course he told you the child isn't his.

TAM: No.

LEE: He didn't tell you the only reason he lets me stay here is that he thinks I'm crazy. He told you about my long distance phone calls.

(TAM *moves to say "no" again but* LEE *continues*.)

LEE: Robbie's waiting for you to shake his hand.

TAM: Hey, this is the wrong movie. I didn't mean to come into no situation.

LEE: That's right, run! I should've known. All afraid of the pretty girls? But oh so anxious to do the right thing—avoid trouble— save face. Look at you so stoic, and that dumb little smile. Do ya talk in giggles too? Are you going to shake my son's hand or not?

TAM: Wanna fuck?

LEE: Yeah.

TAM: Oh, wow, Kenji, you've really grown up!

KENJI: What's wrong, Lee?

LEE: I can't stand people who are rude to children.

KENJI: You're tired, babe.

LEE: I am tired.

TAM: I'm tired and dirty . . . filthy . . . hungry.

LEE: Not too tired to be polite to my son.

KENJI: Oh, hey, man, that's right. You need a bath, right?

TAM: Sure. Hey, kid . . .

LEE: His name is Robbie.

TAM: Hey, Robbie, gimme five!

(TAM *lifts his hand to slap with* ROBBIE, *but* LEE *stops them*.)

LEE: No, not that! It's sick of you to make fun of blacks . . . the way you walk . . . your talk . . . giving five. Who do you think you are?

(TAM *and* ROBBIE *shake hands,* TAM *turning to* LEE *saying* . . .)

TAM: You black?

LEE *and* ROBBIE: No.

TAM: I didn't think so.

LEE: I was married to a black for awhile.

TAM: You had to tell me, didn't ya? Couldn't let me guess. You gave up Janet for this girl, eh Kenji?

LEE: No, I'm not his girl. I'm his good deed.

KENJI: Here, drop your jacket, man.

TAM: I need some coffee. Coffee. I mean coffee! Gotta be bright for my man. Remember that night we were out with Ovaltine the Dancer? He sends ya his love, man. Where is that boy? he said. We're in his life story.

KENJI: Oh, hey . . . you gonna put it in the movie? I'm gonna be on T.V.?

TAM: Movie's gonna turn on two things man, double action, right? That title defense against Claude Dupree he did in his forties. His greatest fight, right? One. And Two how his daddy, Charley Popcorn, made him be that kind of fighter. You should see some of the stuff we shot, man.

KENJI: Yeah. You been on the case then.

TAM: Month in Oakland, our Oakland, shooting background and re-creating the atmosphere of the Dupree fight, after a month with the Dancer, livin with him, man fifty hours of him blabbing his life out on quarter inch tape. And I got the rights to the film of that title defense against Dupree. But it's the Dancer's father, man, Charley Popcorn that's gonna make this movie go. Remember how Ovaltine the Dancer carried on about his mighty daddy? Well, he's here in Pittsburgh man, and we're gonna see him!

KENJI: Yeah!

(TAM *and* KENJI *exchange five*. TAM *grabs a handful of cake crumbs from the table during his speech*.)

TAM: We'll see this Popcorn later, ya know. No equipment on us, right? Nothin to scare him, sound him. Whoo. This child done been hisself up two days, seeing the last of the stuff we shot through the lab, and auditioning the tapes of his Popcorn stories. Now, I'm primed!

KENJI: Maybe you better grab some winks, man, or you won't have no juice to run on later, you know . . .

TAM: No, no, man. If I sleep now, I won't ever wake up. No, I came wired to meet Popcorn, just for a little bit, tonight, check out his pornie house as a possible location, right? And I'm gonna do it, like in that song, they say (TAM *and* KENJI):

SOMEWHERE OVER THE RAINBOW
BLUEBIRDS FLY
BIRDS FLY . . .

(TAM *and* KENJI *exchange five and laugh. Crumbs fall from* TAM's *hand.*)

LEE: You're getting crumbs all over the floor. Why don't you hang up your clothes? I was making curtains there.

TAM: I put his . . .

KENJI: Oh . . .

LEE: Where do you think you are? This place is depressing enough without your mess . . . so dark and unhappy, and that awful noise outside night and day. What is that noise? It's worse today.

KENJI: Sounds like the end of World War 3.

TAM: It's the railroad, they're making up a train down in the yard.

LEE: You're only saying that because you're Chinese.

(TAM *turns ugly a moment, ready to mess her up, then shrugs it off.*)

TAM: I'll pick up the crumbs, okay? And I'll hang up the clothes. Just show me where . . .

LEE: The closets are full.

KENJI: Just leave your stuff, man. Go take your wash and I'll talk to Lee here, okay?

TAM: Yeah.

(ROBBIE *shows* TAM *the way to the bathroom.*)

TAM: Yeah, kid, tasty cake.

ROBBIE: I'll have a piece cut for you when you're done.

(TAM *stalls in the bathroom waiting for* ROBBIE *to leave. Instead* ROBBIE *settles himself in the doorway.* TAM *finally begins stripping down to his shorts. He wears boxer type swimming trunks.*)

KENJI: Why're you acting like this?

LEE: How?

KENJI: Either be nice to my friend or shut up.

ROBBIE: You like kids. I can tell.

TAM: Kenji . . . he your dad?

ROBBIE: No. He hasn't been. You talk loud when you get mad, did you know that?

TAM: You talk funny for a kid, did you know that?

ROBBIE: I've been around. Kenji says you write movies and stuff. You don't look like you'd write kidstuff though.

TAM: Kenji say I write kidstuff? I don't think my stuff is kidstuff.

ROBBIE: That's what I mean. You don't write kidstuff. Maybe I'll be a writer and write movies . . . (TAM *and* ROBBIE) and stuff . . .

TAM: Why don't you talk kidstuff? A man should be a kid when he's a kid. You don't wanna be old all your life . . .

ROBBIE: Lee says a man should fight. But Lee isn't a man, is she.

TAM: Well, people said I never talked like a kid either . . . used to give me quarters for my pearl-studded palaver like I was a kind of jukebox. Take it from me, kid. Talk like a kid while you're a kid, even if you have to fake it.

ROBBIE: Kenji just tells me to shut up.

TAM: I'm sure he has his reasons. Right, kid?

ROBBIE: He doesn't like people to talk to him.

TAM: You talk too much, kid. Cool it and just ask "Why?" and "How-come?"

ROBBIE: How come you're wearing swimming trunks?

TAM: Funny you should ask me that. This is my secret suit! Whenever I see someone in distress I strip down to my secret suit, put up my dukes, and go swimming.

ROBBIE (*laughs*): Nobody tells me jokes like that.

TAM: Maybe it's because nobody likes you! No. No. Forget I said that, kid. See, you talk like a little man long enough and I talk back at you like a man. But you can take it, right? You been around.

ROBBIE: Nobody talks to me like a man. That isn't really your secret suit, is it. I mean, I'm not bothering you am I?

TAM: Naw, it's something I picked up from an old dishwasher who was afraid of white old ladies peeking at him through the keyhole. True! I swear! You see, we had the kitchen in this old folks resthome thing. He thought all them old toothless goofy white

ladies was all for peeking at his body, so he used to wear his un-
derpants right in his bath. Crazy old dishwasher. Sometimes I'd
wash his back, you know. But he was crazy about boxing.

ROBBIE: I'd help my father in his bath too.

TAM: Oh, you did? Must've been old, huh and . . . oh, I see, died
and you and your mom, you came . . . Listen, I'm sorry . . .

ROBBIE: I mean, if I had a father I'd help him like you helped yours.

TAM: He wasn't my father. He was just a crazy old dishwasher.

ROBBIE: But he took care of you.

TAM: I took care of him. He couldn't get around outside of Chinatown without me. All he did for me was take me and Kenji to
fights. He'd go anywhere to catch a fight. Otherwise he was crazy.
He depended on my English, my bad Chinese, was what he was
doing, like when I had to take him to the police to get a form filled
out for the Immigration. Nothin serious. I didn't know that. He
didn't know that, scared.

ROBBIE: You dropped your soap.

TAM: How old are you?

ROBBIE: Eleven. Twelve. Almost twelve. You okay?

TAM: When we got home he said he had to have a bath. He said I
had to help him. I don't remember what kind of language he was
using. I should though don't you think?

ROBBIE: I don't know.

TAM: Neither do I . . . You could see his veins like snakes swimming
in rosewater.

ROBBIE: You okay?

TAM: You ever see real rosewater?

ROBBIE: No.

TAM: I helped him into his bath, and he died. It was just lights out.
He finished it. Do you believe that, kid?

ROBBIE: Yes.

TAM: See what I mean? Now I tell it dry eyed, and I'm believed. I
told it the same at the tub when they came, and they didn't believe me. Because I didn't cry. They got mad. They said I
wouldn't get a quarter. I wasn't tellin a story . . . You know what I
mean?

ROBBIE: No.

TAM: I mean, act your age, kid! Don't talk to me like a little man. I'm not your buddy. I'm an old dude who tells kids jokes, bosses 'em around gruffly, rough houses 'em, has a swell time, and forgets 'em, cuz that's what adults do. Now, do me a favor and get me my case, will ya? And tell your mother I know what trains sound like cuz I used to work on the railroad . . . No, don't. Just get my case, okay?

ROBBIE: . . . and I'll cut you some cake.

(ROBBIE *goes to get case and cut a piece of cake in the kitchen.*)

LEE: What were you two talking about in there?

ROBBIE: Uhh . . . somebody he knew. A Chinese dishwasher who took baths wearing a swimsuit.

LEE: Why don't you like being Chinese, Tam?

TAM: I'm in the bath.

KENJI: Goddamit, Lee, shut up.

LEE: I said, why don't you like being Chinese, Tam? (*To* KENJI) I know he's your childhood friend, but you're not children anymore.

(ROBBIE *returns to bathroom with* TAM's *case and cake. He sets them inside and hangs around the doorway.*)

TAM: What'd you say, Lee?

(KENJI *and* LEE *exchange glances.*)

KENJI: Nothing, man. Be sure to wash under your arms.

ROBBIE: You're Chinese, aren't you? I like Chinese people.

TAM: Me too. They're nice and quiet aren't they?

ROBBIE: One of my fathers was Chinese, like you. He was nice. The nicest.

TAM: Fathers?

ROBBIE: A white one. A Chinese one. One was black. We talk with them on the phone. I liked the Chinese . . . Lee says he wasn't a man.

TAM: Whaddaya mean, Chinese like me and not a man? You some kind of racist midget trying to ride for half fare?

ROBBIE: Should I have said that? Are you mad at me? I don't think you should have told me about the crazy old dishwasher, but I understand. I'm not mad at you.

TAM: Listen, kid. Man to man. If I could be mad at you, I would. I'm not mad at you. But don't talk to me. Your idea of kid talk is just too strange for me.

ROBBIE: Why?

TAM: Ah, now! There's the kid . . . That's all, "Why?" "Why?" Say, "Why?" kid.

ROBBIE: Why?

TAM: You got it.

LEE: What's he doing here anyway? Tell me again, please. I'm listening carefully this time.

KENJI: Aww, Lee! I seeya. I hearya. You don't have to . . .

LEE: Well, what is he doing here?

KENJI: He's making some kind of documentary movie about Ovaltine Jack Dancer, an ex-champion of the light heavyweights. The Dancer's daddy lives here, and Tam's here to see him.

LEE: That's boxing isn't it?

KENJI: Yeah, and don't make anything of that! This could be Tam's big chance.

LEE: Is this boxer Chinese? Of course not, he's black.

KENJI: Yeah.

LEE: I hate people making it on the backs of black people. I don't like your friend at all.

KENJI: But you made it on your back under blacks, and that's okay, huh?

LEE: That's not good grammar. I don't understand what you're saying. But I think you meant to be cruel. You've never been cruel to me before.

KENJI: Listen, Lee.

LEE: You're being cruel to me. You're going to scold me.

KENJI: No, Lee . . . I was going to say I can see what you mean. But I think you're wrong too. About Tam, I mean. And me faking blackness.

LEE: . . . Not you . . .

KENJI: Yeah, me. I mean, Ovaltine Jack the Dancer was our hero, you know. We met him.

LEE: Oh, a story. That's what I need right now, a story.

KENJI: I'm explaining something. Maybe we act black, but it's not fake. Oakland was weirdness. No seasons. No snow. I was a kid missing the concentration camps . . . the country with just us, you know what I mean. Now it's blacks and Chinese all of a sudden. All changed. My folks, everybody . . .

LEE: And you? The young prince returned from exile in the wilderness? Turned black! Presto change-o!

KENJI: I changed! Yeah! Presto! School was all blacks and Mexicans. We were kids in school, and you either walked and talked right in the yard, or got the shit beat outa you every day, ya understand? But that Tam was always what you might say . . . "The Pacesetter." Whatever was happenin with hair, or the latest color, man . . . Sometimes he looked pretty exotic, you know, shades, high greasy hair, spitcurls, purple shiny shirt, with skull cufflinks and Frisko jeans worn like they was fallin off his ass. Me, I was the black one. "BlackJap Kenji" I used to be called and hated yellowpeople. You look around and see where I'm livin, Lee, and it looks like I still do, Pittsburgh ain't exactly famous for no Chinatown or Li'l Tokyo, you know.

LEE: "BlackJap"? I've always thought of you as just plain Kenji . . . a little sullen . . . a little shy.

KENJI: I'm explaining something, okay?

LEE: I was just commenting . . .

KENJI: Okay?

LEE: Okay.

KENJI: Okay. When we were in college, we kidnapped Ovaltine. I mean, Tam did. Tricked him out of his hotel room, and we took him driving out of Oakland and all stood out by the car pissing in the bushes. And I remembered I'd been to New Orleans and, you know, stuck over on the colored side. And I had to piss, and didn't know which way to go. And this black dishwasher there, *saw my plight* so to speak, and took me out to the can and we took places at urinals right next to each other. I thought that was pretty friendly. And I wanted to tell Ovaltine, you know, but Ovaltine being black, might not understand a yellow man, standing next to him, pissing in the bushes, talking about the last memorable time he went pissing with a black man . . . He talked about pissing with the black dishwasher in New Orleans like it was him that did it.

LEE: Sounds just like him.

KENJI: You don't know him.

LEE: Didn't that piss you off? What'd you do?

KENJI: No, I wasn't pissed off. I was glad. I didn't have the guts to do it, you know. He took the risks.

LEE: Ahh. But he's a charlatan, and you're for real.

TAM: No, lass, I'm a charlatan, and he's for real.

LEE: Have you been eavesdropping?

TAM: No, I've been eavesdropping. Me and Robbie ran out of conversation. So since Kenji was tellin all my stories.

KENJI: What's this thing of his about talkin in the bathroom anyway? Every time I go in there he comes to stand in the doorway. What is that?

LEE: Didn't you do that as a boy?

TAM: Where we come from boys who hung around watchin men in the pisser were considered a little funny that way, you know.

LEE: It takes one to know one. *You know.*

KENJI: Lee, what is this all about? Badmouthing my friend, someone you've never seen before, putting me down through him . . . I explained . . . !

LEE: I never put you down!

KENJI: The hell you didn't! I'm not imitating no black people. I'm no copycat. I know I live with 'em, I talk like 'em, I dress . . . maybe even eat what they eat and don't mess with, so what if I don't mess with other Orientals . . . Asians, whatever, blah blah blah. Hell, the way you been talkin to Tam, who's my brother, Lee, you make everything I do sound ugly, man, like I hate myself. And you got no right to say that about me.

LEE: I never said that. I've never seen you like this before.

KENJI: I've never been like this before. I'm with my friend, and in my house with my friend. I should be proud of my house with my friend in here, but you're making me ashamed. And I won't have it. You can mess around with this place anyway you want . . . put up curtains, I don't care. I like 'em. But you're just a guest here. You're not my woman or my lover or nothing but a guest. Now you act like one, you understand?

LEE: I never put you down.

KENJI: You put me down. Damn, you put me down! Bringin in this goddam tatami grassmat Japanese bullshit and knockin the legs off the table . . .

LEE: I just thought . . .

KENJI: You just thought like some little white bitch with the art-books. I'm not Japanese! Tam ain't no Chinese! And don't give me any of that "If-you-don't-have-that-Oriental-culture,-baby,-all-you've-got-is-the-color-of-your-skin" bullshit. But we're not getting into no silk robes and walk around like fools for you!

LEE: You're talking an awful lot!

TAM: Oh, um . . .

KENJI: Yeah, I am, huh. I must be happy.

LEE: Tom's coming.

KENJI: Never heard of him.

LEE: My ex-husband.

KENJI: Ex-husbands and kids. You have so many. White, yellow, black. What is this, Twenty Questions?

LEE: If you'd stop interrupting . . .

KENJI: I'm trying to avoid significant pauses. This conversation has got to have some flow, some pop, some rhythm, or I'm . . .

LEE: He's Chinese . . . The Chinese husband I had, and he says he's coming to take me back to San Francisco with him. He wants my baby.

KENJI: What baby? You been on the phone again with baby news?

LEE: And I'm mad and I'm scared . . . and it isn't easy for me.

TAM: Wow!

LEE: He's a writer.

TAM: What's he write, art books? Chinese cookbooks?

LEE: He's writing a book called *Soul on Rice*.

KENJI *and* TAM: SOUL ON RICE?

TAM: He think that title up all by himself, or did you help?

LEE: I'll tell ya how he thought it up . . .

TAM: No! Don't tell me. Just tell me, is it white rice or brown rice? Must be a cookbook.

KENJI *and* TAM: WILD RICE!

(TAM *and* KENJI *exchange five.* LEE *is laughing in spite of herself.*)

TAM: Yeah, he didn't fulfill your lesbian fantasies. Or was it you found out you didn't like girls? So you left him for a black . . . but then, if he gave you this kid . . .

LEE It's not his!

KENJI: It's not mine.

TAM: All right, immaculate conception. But, for him to think so, you musta given him another chance . . . Lemme see your eyes.

(LEE *turns from* TAM.)

LEE: I don't like being bossed.

TAM: All these husbands and children, man. All colors and decorator combinations. A one woman Minority of the Month Club. Now to Africa, wow . . .

LEE: You're supposed to be comforting me. This is serious.

TAM: Whoowhee! Chinamans do make lousy fathers. I know. I have one.

LEE: How can you laugh at a thing like that?

TAM: I reminded you of your Chinese husband.

LEE: Well, I . . .

TAM (*teasingly*): Huh? Come on, admit it.

LEE: Tam.

TAM: Huh? Yeah?

LEE: Not exactly, maybe . . .

TAM: We all look alike.

LEE: Not exactly, but . . .

TAM: It's okay. You remind me of somebody, too. So we're even. But that's okay. This trip's going to make me well. I'm going to see again, and talk and hear . . . And I got a solution to all your problems. Don't bother with no Twenty Questions, Ouija Board, I Ching or any of that. One: I'm splitting to take care of business. And two: If you don't want to see people, keep the door locked.

KENJI: We'll go see Charley Popcorn, and Lee, if you don't wanta see Tom, keep the door locked. We'll be back soon, Tam's tired . . .

LEE: Why do you have to go? Let Tam go.

TAM: Yeah, I gotta see Charley Popcorn.

LEE: And you and me and Robbie can stay home with the door locked.

KENJI: But I want to see Charley Popcorn too. Father of a champion, man.

LEE: Oh, he's Ovaltine Jack Dancer's father.

TAM: The madman behind the badman! Come on, if you're gonna come on, man. Let's go someplace where we can talk and grab some eats before we see Popcorn.

LEE: Aren't you going to eat here?

TAM: I don't want to eat here!

LEE: But Robbie's been cooking for all of us . . .

TAM: Then you and him eat for all of us. I'm sorry. We hit it off wrong. Maybe under different circumstances . . . like in a dark alley.

LEE: You wouldn't joke like that if you had kids of your own.

TAM: I have two, Sarah and Jonah, named for Sarah and Jonah, remember, Kenji?

LEE: Your wife was white of course.

KENJI: What's color got to do with it? Right, Tam?

TAM: Man, you got it all down, don't ya? Yes, she was white!

LEE: I knew you hated being Chinese. You're all chicken! Not an ounce of guts in all of you put together! Instead of guts you have . . . all that you have is is . . . culture! Watery paintings, silk, all that grace and beauty arts and crafts crap! You're all very pretty, and all so intelligent. And . . . you couldn't even get one of your own girls, because they know . . .

TAM: Know what?

LEE: They know all about you, mama's boys and crybabies, not a man in all your males . . . so you go take advantage of some stupid white girl who's been to a museum, some scared little ninny with visions of jade and ancient art and being gently cared for.

TAM: You're not talking about me.

KENJI: Lee, you're not talking about Tam.

LEE: I am talking about Tam. Tampax Lum, your friend. He's the worst kind. He knows he's no kind of man. Look at him, he's like those little vulnerable sea animals born with no shells of their own so he puts on the shells of the dead. You hear him when he talks? He's talking in so many goddamn dialects and accents all mixed up at the same time, cracking wisecracks, lots of oh yeah, wisecracks, you might think he was a nightclub comic. What'sa wrong with your Chinatowng acka-cent, huh?

KENJI: Lee.

TAM: I got tired of people correcting it. They were even telling me I was "mispronouncing" my name . . . kept telling me it was pronounced "Tom."

LEE: See? More wisecracks. You're just saying that.

TAM: Yeah, that's all I am. And they said I had rags in my mouth, which led to ragmouth, which ended up Tampax. But I hear something in your tongue . . . that funny red in the hair . . . You got the blood don't ya. You're Chinese, right? A breath of the blood?

(LEE *turns away.*)

TAM: Did your Tom know? You were giving Chinamans a chance to smack up skin to skin . . . goin home to yellowness. No, I'm not puttin you down. I'm not arguing with you one bit. Bout nothin. You're right. Everything you say is right. I'm a good loser. I give up.

LEE: Well, don't, can't you get mad? Can't you fight?

TAM: For what? My country? The Alamo? And don't say my "soul." Anyway you're the wrong woman to ask me that. I'd like to hug you for askin though.

LEE: Why don't you?

(TAM *spreads his arms, rises, seems about to move to embrace* LEE, *then shakes himself and sits and holds his head. He takes on some kind of white or European accent and says* . . .)

TAM: "I've known many many women. But with you I'm afraid."

LEE: Come on, I'm just one of the boys.

KENJI: Good! Let's all go out by the car and piss in the bushes.

LEE: Do you see your kids?

KENJI: Well, I'm hungry . . .

TAM: Do you see yours?

KENJI: I'll give Robbie a hand.

LEE: I can't. I want to but . . .

TAM: I can't either. I don't want to. I want 'em to forget me.

LEE: You can't mean that. They're your kids! You can't turn your back on them.

TAM: My back's all that's good for them. My front's no good. Which one was Chinese? Your mother or your father? Grandmother?

Grandfather . . . ? Hmmm? With me in their lives, they'd grow
up to be like you.

LEE: Don't you miss them? I miss my children. Robbie isn't enough.
Sometimes I even miss their fathers.

TAM: I mean, we grow up bustin our asses to be white anyway . . . "Don't wear green because it makes you look yellow,
son." Now there's Confucius in America for you. "Don't be seen
with no blacks, get good grades, lay low, an apple for the teacher,
be good, suck up, talk proper, and be civilized." I couldn't be
friends with Kenji in the open man until . . . I mean, it took us
years after the war to finally not be scared of whitefolks mixing us
up with Japs . . . When I went out, I told the folks I was goin to
visit Mexicans and we didn't feature Mexicans and I was really
running with BlackJap. BlackJap and Tampax, the Ragmouth—for
my fancy yakity yak don't ya know. The Lone Ranger and Tonto of
all those hot empty streets that got so hot in the summer, the
concrete smelled like popcorn and you could smell the tires of
parked cars baking. And what made the folks happiest was for
some asshole, some white offthewall J.C. Penney's clerk type
with his crispy suit to say I spoke English well.

LEE: You're talking too fast for me. I can't . . .

TAM (*continuing through* LEE's *interruptions*): And praisin me for
being "Americanized" and no juvenile delinquency. "The strong
Chinese family . . . Chinese culture." And the folks just
smiled. The reason there was no juvenile delinquency was
because there was no kids! The laws didn't let our women in . . .

LEE: What's this got to do with anything?

TAM: . . . and our women born here lost their citizenship if they
married a man from China. And all our men here, no women,
stranded here burned all their diaries, their letters, everything
with their names on it . . . threw the ashes into the
sea . . . hopin that that much of themselves could find someplace friendly. I asked an old man if that was so. He told me it
wasn't good for me to know such things, to let all that stuff die
with the old.

LEE: You taking me to school?

TAM: He told me to forget it . . . to get along with "Americans."

Well, they're all dead now. We laugh at 'em with the "Americans," talk about them saying "Buck buck bagaw" instead of "giddyup" to their horses and get along real nice here now, don't we?

LEE: Oh, Tam, I don't know.

TAM: I've given my folks white grandkids, right? I don't want 'em to be anything like me, or know me, or remember me. This guy they're calling "daddy" . . . I hear he's even a better writer than me.

KENJI: Who said that? I'll kill him.

LEE: Who said that?

TAM: My mother, tellin me I was no good, to cheer me up. "Brabra," she said. She could never say, "Barbara." It was always "Brabra" like . . . (TAM *hefts imaginary boobs*.) You know there's a scientific relation between boobs and ambition. I'm not greedy for boobs. No ambition. I'm just gonna make this movie. Keep busy. Just do one thing right, right? That Ovaltine-Dupree fight! Damn! He was so happy Ovaltine the Dancer won. I bought into this movie to do it right, with money I should be usin for the child support. I even begged some up from the folks. Lots of home cooking and playing a goodboy listenin to his ma, for his "allowance."

LEE: See? You do care.

TAM: I even took a grubstake from you, eh, Kemo Sabay. You scared?

KENJI: My silver bullets, your silver bullets, Masked Man.

TAM: My kids might see it some day, and . . . And they'll see . . .

LEE: You see, Tam? You can't turn your back on them. You don't mean it when you say you want them to forget you.

TAM: I mean it. I mean, in case they don't forget. I should leave them something . . . I should have done some THING. One thing I've done alone, with all my heart. A gift. Not revenge. But they've already forgotten me. They got a new, ambitious, successful, go-for-bucks, superior white daddy.

LEE: Tam, you bastard, you make me so pissed. You could be a wonderful father. No! No! I won't let Tom take this baby for his rich bitch mother again.

KENJI: Huh?

LEE: You won't make me see him. Don't talk about it. Don't even talk about it.

TAM (*interrupting*): I was talking about ambition! They say a man with an old lady with big tits is ambitious. The bigger the tits on his lady, the greater the ambition. "Brabra" didn't have any tits at all. She had depressions, like two bomb craters in the chest. And ma said, "Brabra" . . . NO, it was, "*Son,* Brabra must like writers, only Rex is successful." *I bet her tits are bigger now.* But ma seemed so pleased about it. That "I told you so" tone, as if she'd got her revenge on me, as if she'd known all my life I was no good and was just waiting to tell me . . . Kenji, stop me, I'm stealing your girl with cheap woo.

KENJI: Sounds like pretty deluxe woo to me. I've been taking notes.

LEE: I'm not his girl. I'm his guest. He says he won't touch white girls.

KENJI: Not me, too scary.

TAM: Man, Lee's not white.

KENJI: I didn't hear it from her.

TAM: She's chicken to say it. Help her out.

KENJI: Aww, man, if I'm going to go to all the trouble of mind to get a white girl, man, she's going to be all white. And tall. And giant, huge tits man. And blonde. The scariest kind of white girl there is, man, none of this working my way up for me. Blonde hairs all over her head. Tall . . . and tits, man like when I walk up to her and get my little nose stuck in her navel, man, and I look up at her belly, I feel like I'm on the road with you and see two Giant Orange stands across the road from each other.

TAM: Yeah, do it. You got ambition. No down in the cellar for Helen Keller for Kenji.

KENJI: I'm chicken.

TAM: If you were blonde and had these big tits, Kenji could . . .

KENJI: No, I'd chicken out. I'm chicken.

TAM: We're all chicken.

LEE: No one here but us chickens.

TAM: It's like that inspired wino sittin on the crapper in the T&D Theatre in old Oakland wrote on the wall (KENJI *listens with growing recognition*):

"When Chickencoop Chinaman have wetdream far from home,
      He cly Buck buck bagaw, squeezing off his bone."

TAM *and* KENJI: Longfellow.

LEE (*overlapping* TAM *and* KENJI): Buck buck bagaw?

(TAM *and* KENJI *pound up a rhythm on glasses, the tabletop, anything handy.* LEE *stamps her feet. They whinny, grunt, squeak, moan, come on like a screaming jungle at night full of animals.*)

KENJI: A fiery horse with the speed of light, a cloud of dust and a hearty . . .

ALL: BUCK BUCK BAGAW . . . THE CHICKENCOOP CHINAMAN!

(*All begin singing Buck Buck Bagaw to the* William Tell *Overture and pounding on things. The tune goes out of their voices and they're screaming noise, throwing in an occasional "Buck Buck Bagaw!" This isn't singing but a kind of vocal athletic event.*)

TAM: "If you don't have Chinese culture, baby, all you've got is the color of your skin."

ALL: BUCK BUCK BAGAW.

KENJI: "How do you tell Chinks from Japs?"

ALL: BUCK BUCK BAGAW.

(*The music becomes frantic, full of screams and whoops and lots of beating on things.* KENJI *grabs coins from his pockets and throws them at the wall. He stamps empty tin cans flat. He and* ROBBIE *howling and screaming take pots and pans out of the cupboard and beat on them awhile, get bored and throw them across the room, and get others.* LEE *pounds on the table as hard as she can with her fists, beating up a rhythm, throwing the curtain material on the floor.* TAM *puts down the guitar and goes to the bathroom and turns on the shower taps, making the pipes shudder . . . and comes back to beat on cups, bottles, glasses with a spoon. All intermittently cry "Buck Buck Bagaw" and all answer with a cry of "Buck Buck Bagaw!"*)

TAM: Hey. Let's all go see Charley Popcorn at his pornie house! Give him a family.

ALL: BUCK BUCK BAGAW.

KENJI: We'll leave that Tom in the cold.

(*Enter* ROBBIE *from the kitchen*.)
ROBBIE: Dinner's ready.
ALL: BUCK BUCK BAGAW.

[*Curtain*]

ACT TWO

SCENE ONE

Blackout and fade-in spot on TAM *downstage center. Second spot on* KENJI *tuning a large old-fashioned radio.*

TAM: Did ya hear that . . . ? Listen, children, did I ever tellya, I ever tellya the Lone Ranger ain't a Chinaman? I ever tellya that? Don't blame me. That's what happens when you're a Chinaman boy in the kitchen, listening in the kitchen to the radio, for what's happenin in the other world, while grandmaw has an ear for nothing but ancient trains in the night, and talks pure Chinamouth you understood only by love and feel. She don't hear what a boy hears. She's for the Chinese Hour and chugablood red roving, livin to hear one train, once more. I heard JACK ARMSTRONG, ALL-AMERICAN BOY fight Japs, come outa the radio everyday into our kitchen to tell me everyday for years that ALL-AMERICAN BOYS are the best boys, the hee-rohs! the movie stars! that ALL-AMERICAN BOYS are white boys everyday, all their life long. And grandmaw heard thunder in the Sierra hundreds of miles away and listened for the Chinaman-known Iron Moonhunter, that train built by Chinamans who knew they'd never be given passes to ride the rails they laid. So of all American railroaders, only they sung no songs, told no jokes, drank no toasts to the ol' iron horse, but stole themselves some iron on the way, slowly stole up a pile of steel, children, and hid there in the granite face of the Sierra and builded themselves a wild engine to take them home. Every night, children, grandmaw listened in the kitchen, waiting, til the day she died. And I'd spin the dial looking for to hear ANYBODY, CHINESE AMERICAN BOY, ANYBODY, CHINESE AMERICAN BOY anywhere on the dial, doing anything grand on the air, anything at all. . . . I heard of the masked man. And I listened to him. And in the Sunday funnies he had black hair, and Chinatown was nothin but black hair, and for years, listen, years! I grew blind looking hard through the holes of his funnypaper mask for slanty eyes. Slanty eyes, boys! You see, I knew, children, I knew with all my heart's insight . . . shhh, listen, children . . . he wore that mask to hide his Asian eyes! And that made sense of me. I knew he wore a red shirt for good luck. I knew he rode a white horse named Silver cuz white be our color of death. Ha ha ha. And he was lucky Chinaman vengeance on the West . . . and silver bullets cuz death from a Chinaman is always expensive. Always classy. Always famous. I knew the Lone Ranger was the CHINESE AMERICAN BOY of the radio I'd looked for.

(*Music up: Rossini's* William Tell *Overture. Spot picks up* LONE RANGER *and* TONTO *on toy horses. The* RANGER *and* TONTO *are both old and decrepit.* RANGER *takes out a six-gun and struggles to take aim at* TAM's *hand.*)

TAM: . . . And I tuned him in! And listened in the kitchen for the Ranger to bring me home. (TAM *raises his right hand as if giving an oath.*) And I kept his secrets.

(RANGER *fires, says* . . .)

RANGER: Kapow! Right in the hand . . .

(RANGER *rides off cackling and wheezing. Music down and out.*)

TAM (*narratively, still in reflection, points at his hand and says*): He shot me in the hand. (*Terrified and in pain*) He shot me in the hand! (*Narratively*) I shouted, and this old, old Indian in rotten buckskins . . .

RANGER: Easy, big fella . . .

(TONTO *takes his bow and arrows, follows* TAM, *who moves toward* KENJI. TONTO *moves to a position behind* TAM *and the* RAN- GER . . .)

TAM: . . . got behind his mouse, aimin his bow'n'arrow at me and shouted, "Hey, who was that masked man?"

TONTO: Hey! Who was that masked man?

(TAM *and* KENJI *turn toward* TONTO.)

TAM: What masked man?

TONTO: Louder!

(TAM *and* KENJI *turn toward* RANGER.)

TAM *and* KENJI: That was a masked man?

TONTO: Did you see that white horse?

TAM *and* KENJI (*to* TONTO): What white horse?

TONTO: That white horse named Silver!

TAM *and* KENJI (*to* RANGER): Silver!

TONTO: You see them bullets?

(TAM *and* KENJI *turn toward* TONTO.)

TAM: What bullets?

TONTO: Them *siiilver* bullets, gents!

(TAM *and* KENJI *turn toward* RANGER.)

KENJI: Silver bullets! Yaaahhooh! Hah ha ha. You was shot in the mitt with a silver bullet, ol compadre!

TAM (*to his hand*): Gahhhhhhk! (*To* TONTO) Was he really wearin

TAM *and* KENJI: a mask?

TONTO: Ummmk.

KENJI (*whispers*): That means, "Yes," you lucky dog.

(TONTO *draws back on his bow.*)

TONTO (*shouting*): HEY! Who was that MASKED MAN?

RANGER (*in the distance*): Tonto! What's holdin things up? It's near time for my injection.

TONTO (*sotto voce*): Come on China Boys, just answer the question. (*Shouting*) Hey who was that MASKED MAN?

TAM: Blood!

(KENJI *claps a hand over* TAM's *mouth just as* TONTO *lets fly an arrow that sticks in the radio.*)

KENJI: Why, that must be THE LONE RANGER!

TONTO: . . . And?

TAM: And?

TONTO: . . . And don't you want to thank him? Hurry, man!

KENJI: AND I WANTED TO THANK HIM.

TAM: For shooting me in the hand?

TONTO *and* KENJI: Shhh.

RANGER (*in the distance, shouting*): Come on big fella. (*In the distance*) Hi yo Silver Awayyyy!

KENJI: You lucky sonofabitch!

(*The* LONE RANGER *comes back on a staggering Silver, the* RAN-
GER *stays mounted. He takes off and puts on his hat mechanically,
breathlessly, compulsively muttering "Hi yo Silver, Awayyy!"
perking up and listening for himself, then muttering the shout
again.* TONTO *rushes over to him, rolls up the* RANGER's *sleeve,
puts a tourniquet around his arm, fills a hypo and shoots the* RAN-
GER *up.*)

TAM: Why'd you shoot me in the hand?

RANGER *and* KENJI: Kapow! Right in the hand.

RANGER: Heh hah. (*Doing crazy gun tricks. His voice, and apparent
age, abruptly change from the hero to various fans, to the old
radio announcer.*) Nowhere in the pages of history can one find a
greater/ Why that was the Lone Ranger/Why! I wanted to thank
him/ Hi yo Silver Awayyy! You hear that, Tonto? That
cry . . . He's gone! Listen to them thundering hoofbeats. I
wanted to thank him, Tonto. Hi yo Silver Awayy . . .

(KENJI *gallops and pat-a-cakes his butt around the radio chanting up the Lone Ranger music;* RANGER *runs down* . . .)

TONTO (*without accent*): Right, Kemo Sabay. Get off the horse now,
Silver needs to rest a spell.

RANGER (*cringing*): You're not Tonto! Where's my Kemo Sabay?
Where's my faithful Indian companion? Tonto!

TONTO (*faking accent*): Ummk, Kemo Sabay. You get off horse now.

(TAM *as* TONTO *takes on fake accent, gives a sneering, jeering,
smartass climbing dirty laugh.* KENJI *grins happily.*).

RANGER: There ya are, Tonto. Hi yo . . . Hi yo ssss . . . Hi yo
what, Tonto?

(KENJI *shakes radio* . . .)

TAM: *That* brought law and order to the early western United
States?

RANGER: A FIERY HORSE WITH THE SPEED OF LIGHT, A CLOUD OF DUST,
AND A HEARTY HI YO SILVER!

ALL: THE LONE RANGER!

RANGER: GOD, I LOVE IT! *Nowhere in the pages of history can one find
a greater champion of justice.* You China boys been lucky up to
now, takin it easy, preservin your culture.

TAM *and* KENJI: Huh?

RANGER: . . . Some culture! Look at this shirt! A hero like me needs fast service. I said light starch, and look at this! This is what I tamed the West for? *You hear thundering hoofbeats? Anybody hear thundering hoofbeats?* You better do something about preservin your culture, boys, and light starch! *Hold it! Listen!*

(TAM *and* KENJI *get on their hands and knees and put an ear to the ground and listen for hoofbeats . . .*)

RANGER: *Sounds like galloping out of the pages of history!* You hear? (*To* TAM *and* KENJI *on the floor at* RANGER's *feet*) Lookie that humility, Tonto. I admire it. (*Sits on* TAM's *butt after dusting it off*) You China Boys don't know what it's like ridin off into the distance all your life, and watchin your mouth. Watchin your mouth and ridin off into the distance. Riding off into the night toward the moon on your damned horse screamin away (KENJI *joins in*) Hi Yo Silver, awayyyyyy! / Did you hear that cry? I didn't cotton to riding off into the distance one night screamin that Hi Yo Silver, awayyy / *Ya hear that?* Shhh!

TAM *and* KENJI: NO!

(RANGER *spies microphone, rises, reaches into shirt and takes out a tattered script. He goes to the mike and tosses off pages as he reads.*)

RANGER: It was a pie bakin shindig. And I sure had me a hankerin for some pie. But Tonto and the grateful townfolks what had gotten this function together for me by way of thanks for doing somethin heroic had it all planned. How they'd all be in there *waiting* for me, you know, to *thank* me. And how they would all be in there together grinnin when they'd hear me too shy for pie gallop off and how they'd figger out who I was and how they'd say they wanted to thank me, just before I was off in the distance screamin at my horse! Easy, big fella. HI YO SILVER, AWAYYYY. *You hear that cry?* Well, tonight, I didn't feel like riding off into the distance!

TAM *and* KENJI: No!

(*They pick up radio and shake it.*)

RANGER: This time I wanted some pie. Ala mode too. And I was in love with a piece of local ass.

TAM *and* KENJI: No!

(*They shake the radio.*)

RANGER: Helen was her name too. White Old West translation of them three Chinee monkeys, Hear no Evil, See no Evil, Speak no Evil. Three in one compact model, boys. A blind girl. Stone blind. Deaf too, and dumb! Really give me a kick watchin her bump into things. You should have seen her pie!

TAM *and* KENJI: Yeech!

> (*They shake the radio, roll on the floor, pound the sides of their heads as if trying to get water out of their ears.*)

RANGER: Made it by feel and smell, she did. I sure wanted me a piece of her pie! . . . And I got it / Huh? Was I a bad man, Tonto? Tell me, ol' compadre, Kemo Sabay, good ol' Tonto, was I bad for what I done?

TONTO: Ummk.

KENJI: That means, "Take it easy, Kemo Sabay."

RANGER: I did ride off, didn't I, Tonto? And all the people was in there? And they . . . tell me what Helen . . . Helen What's hername said. I loved her, Tonto, cute as three monkeys. Heh. You hear that? LOVE!

TAM *and* KENJI: Gak! Love!

> (*They gallop around beating their butts.*)

RANGER: She and me were kin in spirit. You hear that? Listen? *I think I hear the galloping hoofbeats of* / COME WITH US NOW AS ONCE AGAIN FROM OUT OF THE PAST / Tonto, tell me what she said again, I like to hear it.

> (TAM *and* KENJI *collapse by radio and listen.*)

TONTO (*without accent*): Well, Jeezis that was a long time ago, old timer. Let's see now, we were . . .

RANGER: Not that way, Tonto. Be yourself. Kemo Sabay me.

TONTO (*fake accent, except when quoting*): She never speakum before. Folks heap surprised, Kemo Sabay, her say, "Hey, who was that masked man?"

> (TAM *and* KENJI *exchange five.* TAM *winces in pain.*)

RANGER (*whispering in a reverie*): "Hey, who was that masked man?"

TONTO: Somebody sayum, "You see them silver bullets?"

> (TAM *and* KENJI *as rolling train wheels . . .*)

RANGER: Hold it. Ya hear that in the distance? Hurry. Get to that part where she said . . .

TONTO: She say with tear in eye, "I wanted to thank him."

RANGER: I wanted to thank him . . .

TONTO: . . . and from far distance we hearum . . .

(TAM *and* KENJI *as whippoorwilling train whistle . . .*)

RANGER: Ya hear that . . . ?

TAM: . . . The Ranger said it were a train. I heard it come spooky, callin over the dark town. The Iron Moonhunter, grandmaw listened for til the day she died . . .

RANGER: You don't hear no train, China boys. Hear no evil, ya hear me? China boys, you be legendary obeyers of the law, legendary humble, legendary passive. Thank me now and I'll let ya get back to Chinatown preservin your culture!

TAM *and* KENJI: Culture.

TAM: You shot me in the hand.

RANGER: Thank me later boys. I hear ya breakin all kinds of law and order, rollin, vengeance after me . . . Me, Tonto! Chinamans with no songs, no jokes, no toasts, and no thanks. China Boys! No thanks for the masked man! Who was that masked man? I wanted to thank him. You think folks really give a hoot to see my eyes? You think I'd still be the Lone Ranger without this here mask? Now you wanta thank me?

TAM: Why'd you shoot me in the hand, old man? I ain't no bad guy.

RANGER: I curse ya honorary white!

TAM *and* KENJI: We don't wanta be honorary white.

RANGER: I'm the law, China Boys, it's a curse I'm a givin ya to thank me for, not a blessing. In your old age, as it were in your legendary childhood, in the name of Helen Keller, Pearl Buck, and Charlie Chan, kiss my ass, know thou that it be white, and go thou happy in honorary whiteness forever and ever, preservin your culture, AMEN.

TAM *and* KENJI: We don't wanta be honorary white.

RANGER: Don't move! Gettum up! Keep your asses off them long steel rails and short cross ties, stay off the track, don't be a followin me, stop chasin me, or you'll be like me, spendin your whole lifetime ridin outa your life into everybody's distance, runnin away from lookin for a train of sullen Chinamans, runaways from their place in the American dream, not thanking me . . . not thanking the masked man . . . the West ain't big enough for the both of us! But, say, ya speak good English, China Boy . . .

TAM: Thank you.

RANGER: He thanked me, Tonto. We can ride now, ol' compadre. Let's ride . . .

TAM: The masked man . . . I knew him better when I never knew him at all. The Lone Ranger ain't no Chinaman, children.

RANGER: Adios, compadres.

> (*Music up on* RANGER's *signal.* TONTO *and* RANGER *mount up and ride off.* KENJI *saunters, grins and waves after them.*)

KENJI: Adios, masked man. Adios! Adios!

RANGER: The Lone Ranger rides again! Hi Yo Silver Away.

TONTO: Get 'em up, Scout!

TAM: He'd deafened my ear for trains all my boyhood long . . .

> [*Curtain*]

SCENE TWO

Porno movie house. Night.

CHARLEY POPCORN *is an old black man, dressed up conservatively flashy in a shiny suit cut a little out of date, pastel shirt, skinny tie, big cuff links, a diamond ring. A knit vest sweater, and incongruous aluminum hardhat and welder's goggles.*

Railroad crashing intermittently in background.

The theater is full of the juicy noises, moaning, whines, shrieks, grunts, creaks, bumps of the pornie soundtrack.

TAM *and* KENJI *in the lobby stare into the auditorium and look slowly from one end of the screen to the other, gaping.*

KENJI: She Chinese or Japanese?

> (KENJI *wears a porkpie hat and shades, an old out-of-date*

jacket with leather patches, a good shirt with long collars, and a wide tie. TAM *dressed dark, trim and slim. No hat. Cowboy boots.)*

POPCORN (*from inside theater*): Hey, you two queers, sit down and hold hands, and don't bother the perverts willya?

TAM: Charley Popcorn?

POPCORN (*entering lobby*): Quiet, man! People payin to hear the sucky fucky. Lotta my clientele is dirty word, sucky fucky sound freaks ya understand?

TAM: Customer's always right.

(POPCORN *is aloof, self-contained and a little shaky with age.* TAM *squirms, waiting for an opening for talk.)*

POPCORN: You want your money back or what?

(POPCORN *takes* TAM *and* KENJI *to office.)*

TAM: No, Mr. Popcorn, I'm Tam Lum. I phoned you from L.A. remember?

POPCORN: Tam Lum?

TAM: . . . about this documentary movie we're making on Ovaltine Jack Dancer . . . ?

POPCORN: Tam Lum? What kind of name is that?

TAM: Chinese.

POPCORN: Sounds Chinese.

TAM: It is Chinese, Mr. Popcorn.

POPCORN: It is Chinese? Here, look at me, here. I be going blind. Eyes hurt, you understand. And I got a hurt in my head. One little bump and I die, ya see? These movies bad for my eyes. But I can't see a uhhh a (*points at screen*) vagina unless it's forty feet acrosst. You gonna put Ovaltine in a movie, huh? Why ya tellin me that? He's been in pictures before.

TAM: No, this is a movie about Ovaltine. We're making a movie *about* his life.

POPCORN: I'm half blind, boy, not half deaf, mind . . .

TAM: Sorry, we're making this movie about Ovaltine Jack Dancer's life, and we're talking to all of his friends and relatives . . .

POPCORN: "We"? Who's "we"?

TAM: Condor Productions and me.

POPCORN: I mean who's in charge?

TAM: I am.

POPCORN: Oh . . . You Chinese?

TAM: I . . .

POPCORN: That a Chinese company? from China?

TAM: No, it's in L.A.

POPCORN: American?

TAM: Yeah.

POPCORN: But you're Chinese.

TAM: I . . .

POPCORN: I don't want to do anything wrong, see? I used to be pretty slick! (*Chuckles reflectively*)

TAM: Yeah, I've heard a lot about you. Ovaltine has. . .

POPCORN: Isn't it strange, you're Chinese.

TAM: I'm a . . . I'm an American citizen.

POPCORN: You don't talk like a Chinese, do ya? No, I don't think so . . .

TAM: I was born here, Mr. Popcorn.

POPCORN: The way you talked, why, I took you for colored over the phone. But "Lum"? Why would a Chinese talk like a colored man?

TAM: Mr. Popcorn, I . . .

POPCORN: You can talk like Mr. Charley too . . .

TAM: I didn't know people still said "Mr. Charley." That's old where I come from.

POPCORN: I am an old man. I'm too old to stand for jokes and signifying. You . . . Ovaltine know you're Chinese?

TAM: Yeah. We're kind of old friends. Me and Kenji, when we were kids, a few years after the Dupree . . .

POPCORN: Who?

TAM: Kenji.

POPCORN: Never heard of him. What's that, "Kenji"? Chinese too?

KENJI: Japanese.

TAM: No, Japanese. He's right here . . .

POPCORN: Oh, Japanese, and you're . . .

TAM: Chinese . . .

POPCORN: You like music? I remember a cute little song about Chinese. American song. I still remember it:

> MY LITTLE HONG KONG DREAM GIRL
> IN EVERY DREAM YOU SEEM, GIRL,
> TWO ALMOND EYES ARE SMILING,
> AND MY POOR HEART IS WHIRLING
> LIKE A BIG SAIL ROUND MY PIGTAIL . . .

You ever hear that before?

TAM: No.

POPCORN: Oh, before your time.

TAM: About Ovaltine, Mr. Popcorn . . .

POPCORN: You know Ovaltine likes music.

TAM (*fumbling*): Uh, yeah, as I was saying, I . . . we took Ovaltine for a ride, went out riding with Ovaltine when he was back in Oakland, uh California, where, you know, before we'd seen the Dupree fight? . . . and, we all got out of the short, the car, and under the stars, we stood next to the car, and on the road, you know, pissed all together into the bushes . . . (*Chuckles.* POPCORN *doesn't react* . . . TAM *and* KENJI *exchange looks.*) We were just kids then, but since then we say . . . it was the greatest . . . saw the Dancer come back and knock out Dupree in the 11th in Oakland, I guess he was our hero . . . He had fond memories of pissing on the, I mean, off the roadside with you . . .

POPCORN: What?

TAM: I guess that was the greatest piss we ever took in our lives, right, Kenji?

KENJI: Yeah, it was a dynamite piss, Mr. Popcorn.

POPCORN: Why you talkin to me about pissin in bushes for? Why is it they want Chinese to make a picture on Ovaltine? I'm not sure about this. Ovaltine know you Chinese are doing a picture on him?

TAM: I guess you don't feature Chinese too much, huh?

POPCORN: "Feature"? I don't know. I don't like 'em though. You asked, and I'm tellin ya. I gotta watch out for the Dancer. He's pretty slick, but . . . (*Shakes his head*) The only Chinese I ever talked to up close with face to face be waiters, I remember . . .

(TAM *moves to speak, but* KENJI *holds him back, saying* . . .)

KENJI: Let 'em talk, man. It's just talk.

POPCORN: They . . . they treated us worse 'n white men treated us. And those Chinese restaurants we went to wasn't fancy. Flies?

TAM: How do you feel about being in a movie about your boy, Mr. Popcorn?

POPCORN: You mean, you want me in the movie?

TAM: Yeah, you gotta be.

POPCORN: What kind o' money am I gonna get for this movie?

TAM: You mean American or Chinese money?

POPCORN: I mean Grants or Franklins?

TAM: Well, this ain't no blockbuster, ya know.

POPCORN: You mean no money?

TAM: There'll be a legal dollar for signing the release, otherwise . . .

POPCORN: No money!

TAM: Ovaltine said you might like a print of the movie, when it's done. You know, somethin to remember him by.

POPCORN: I think I better call him up.

TAM: Don't you trust me? What do you think I'm doin' here?

KENJI: Why don't we leave the man call up Ovaltine?

POPCORN: I just wanta make sure, you know. This all makes me dizzy.

TAM: You think I'm a practical joke or what?

KENJI: You call up Ovaltine, and we'll be outside. We'll pop for the call.

TAM: What're ya doin?

(KENJI *takes* TAM *out of* POPCORN's *office*.)

KENJI: You need some sleep, man.

TAM: He's Ovaltine Jack Dancer's father?

KENJI: What'd you expect, Joe Louis?

TAM: You catch his Man from Mars costume, man? And the nice way he has with yellow people?

KENJI: He's an old man.

TAM: He's a bigot. He's nothin but a black white racist when it comes to yellow people.

KENJI: He's an old man! He knows nothing about us. I mean, what would you do, you pick up the phone and someone's jabberin to you in Chinese, right? Whaddaya expect? And you meet the dude and he's black, and talkin Chinese. Wouldn't that shake you up?

TAM: So ya want me to talk, "Ah-so, Misser Popcorn, Confucius say, Char-reeh Chan"?

KENJI: You're over-reacting.

TAM: Lee's right, man. This is a goddamned minstrel show . . . talk white to the blacks and black to the whites, is that what you're saying. Is that your formula for success in Pittsburgh?

KENJI: Come on, man, you're not listening. Somebody you talked to on the phone soundin Chinese pops up black. Wouldn't that shake you up? Really. Be serious.

TAM: You're saying I'm a bigot.

KENJI: No, man, just listen . . . ! Listen.

TAM: You think I'm a fool. I thought we were friends. Now I find you think I'm a fool.

KENJI: This isn't you, man.

TAM: I thought we were friends, man. I thought you were different. But you're not . . . you're nothin but a . . .

KENJI: Jap dentist?

TAM: Lee's right, you hate yourself. You hate your profession. You're in some kind of fog, man. It really hurt me, hearin you let alla Lee's badmouth on you bout fakin blackness for balls just slip by.

KENJI: She was talkin 'bout you.

TAM: Oh! I thought you had a reason, man. Cuz you always had reasons. Tell me, what's the reason for you runnin a refugee camp for the weird kid and his mother? And you not even sleeping with her. Ooh, and she likes to tell me too. Oh, I hate to see that. But I figure you got a reason. I wouldn't touch her myself.

KENJI: Tam!

TAM: I wouldn't let no bitch bleed me and thank me with badmouth, especially Lee! But you got reasons, right?

KENJI: Right.

TAM: Well what's your reason for thinkin I'm all for laughs?

KENJI: I'm sorry if I lost my temper.

TAM (cold): I never noticed.

KENJI: Hey, I'm on your side. You're tired, man.

TAM: You're the one that's tired, man. Not me. I'm too fast for ya, right?

(*Enter* POPCORN.)

POPCORN: Ovaltine says you're pretty slick, Mr. Lum, and I believe it. I remember his first fight . . . but let me say, first, we both businessmen, right? And maybe we can do some business. Maybe we could premiere that movie right here, invite folks, turn off the fuckshow for a night. Now with just a little money for a new paint job . . .

TAM: Well, Ovaltine said you got him up to hittin the speedbag eight hundred times a minute for the Dupree fight.

POPCORN: Aww, that Ovaltine, he likes to exaggerate, you know what I mean? He bullshits. We won that fight you know how? We bullshit Ovaltine about his age and strength, and he bullshit Dupree. Maybe I told him I timed his hittin the speedbag eight hundred times maybe even nine hundred times a round, but not in no one minute. Most he ever did in one minute, and nobody could keep this up more, I'm telling ya, is three hundred times. And when he could do that, every day, one time, maybe two times, I figured he was ready . . . You know, we had a Chinese used to come watch Ovaltine train for that fight.

TAM: She was beautiful of course.

POPCORN: Old Chinese gentleman. We nicknamed him the "Chinatown Kid." Ovaltine'd see him in the bleachers, and wave, say "Ho, Chinatown Kid," and he'd say, "Too moochie shi-yet." (*Chuckles*) Reason he did that was one day I thought we'd let him in for free so I give him his dollar back, but he didn't understand, see. Me and Ovaltine didn't know that, and every time he stuck the dollar at us, we smiled and shook our heads and pointed inside, but he musta thought we were kickin him out. And he got this look on his face, and he held up his dollar, and we shook our heads, tellin him, you know, he was free. Then he said, I'll never forget it, "Too moochie shi-yet." And he walked away. I felt awful. I chased him down the street and held out my hand, and he gave me the dollar and I took him into the gym again. He had to pay. He would not be free. How bout our business proposition.

TAM: He wore a hat.

POPCORN: No. I don't remember no hat. But I liked to died, when he fierce, fierce! "Too moochie shi-yet!" like that. Then I could see his whole life, you understand?

TAM: A new hat, brushed.

POPCORN: I used to wonder how he ever got to find the gym, you know. No Chinese ever came by. I mean wherever we were training.

TAM: I took him by.

POPCORN: He was your daddy! Why didn't you come up with him?

TAM: No, he wasn't my father. He . . . He wore a hat.

POPCORN: No, no, I don't remember no hats. Maybe it wasn't the same gentleman.

KENJI: Maybe.

TAM: Man, nothing could keep him from boxin. He loved to be called that Chinatown Kid stuff too.

POPCORN: You know his name? Maybe, who knows? . . .

TAM: . . . No. I only heard it once . . . read it in a letter from the immigration. Isn't that strange? Not even at the funeral. I don't remember.

POPCORN: Oh, he passed . . .

TAM: Most of the old folks I knew never had names . . . I can't think of any. So he used to . . .

POPCORN: That don't make sense. What do Chinese call each other then? How can they talk?

TAM: I just called them "uncle," *Ah-bok Ah-sook*, like that. They were afraid of having names here. Afraid America would find 'em and deport 'em.

POPCORN: We called him "The Chinatown Kid."

TAM: I never thought about his name before . . . that's where he got that "Chinatown Kid" thing! Ha . . .

POPCORN: You shoulda come up the stairs with him to the gym.

TAM: Oh, man, he used to shout at me. He'd get scared.

POPCORN: I don't know nothin' 'bout that. I just know it's wrong to turn your back on your father however old you be.

TAM: He wasn't my father. He was . . . he was our dishwasher.

POPCORN: What's wrong with dishwashers?

TAM: Nothin wrong with dishwashers. Uh, listen. I think your story about him would be good in the movie, you know. "The China-town Kid," and the training for the Dupree fight . . . nice side-light . . .

POPCORN: No, this old Chinese gentleman wasn't scared. He had dignity.

TAM: I said he wasn't chicken. But I should know if he was scared or not.

POPCORN: All right.

TAM: All right. Let's forget the old man for the time being. Let's not talk about him . . . but about the movie.

POPCORN: I don't think you should forget the old man.

TAM: You're doing this on purpose. I didn't mean it that way.

POPCORN: Well, that's none of my business I suppose. But I think maybe I respected him more than you . . . and colored people don't particularly favor Chinese, you know . . . I'm just tellin ya. You wouldn't want me to lie.

TAM: What do you know about it?

POPCORN: Maybe he was scared for you . . . It's none of my business.

TAM: No one respected him more than me.

POPCORN: That's none of my business. (*To* KENJI) Oh, I was gonna tellya about Ovaltine's first fight, talkin of yellow Negroes . . . Now I'm not callin you no yellow Negroes, but it makes ya easier to think about, ya understand?

Long time ago, back in the depression days. Ovaltine was just a youngster then, and it was one of those out of doors matches. There was oil drum fires all around the ring. Coldsnap, you understand? Back in Ohio, coldsnap. Wouldya like some coffee or somethin, Mr. Lum?

TAM (*mumbles*): No, thanks.

POPCORN: Well, Ovaltine was fightin this big old yellow Negro man, older fella. A real tanker. He was yellow as a schoolbus, yellow as beer piss . . . This the kinda story you want me to tell?

KENJI: Was it a good fight?

POPCORN: Good fight?

TAM: We'll put it in the movie. You tellin it, and we seein it . . .

POPCORN: This old gentleman had a punch that wouldn't crack an egg.

TAM: Yeah, I see it.

POPCORN: Ovaltine stepped in and beat on him, hit him, jabs, right cross, left cross, uppercut, to the body, everywhere and it was like he was trying to knock down a haystack with his fists. The tanker just stood his self there and would not fall. Finally, after bout maybe twelve rounds, Ovaltine just wore his self out from all the dancin and prancin punchin and sockin and fell down in a faint. He done knocked hisself out. But I saw the talent, the natural timing, and the mean, I mean, smart, thinking mean, like a killer. That's how me and Ovaltine come to meet.

TAM (*snapping*): Hey!

POPCORN: You like that?

TAM: What do you mean, that's how you and Ovaltine came to meet?

POPCORN: I never see'd that boy before. Soon's he got up from his faint, his sweat all froze on his body and hair too, he said, first thing, grinning like, "I did enjoy the fight so very much."

KENJI: That's what he said after the Dupree fight.

POPCORN: That's what he said after EVERY fight!

TAM: Yeah, yeah. he said that after every fight, but he said you taught him to do that when he was a kid in Mississippi.

POPCORN: Mississippi? What Mississippi? He was sixteen . . . seventeen when I ever first saw him. In Ohio that day!

TAM: Hey, I don't know what's happenin between you and the Dancer, that's none of my business, but I read, and Ovaltine himself told me . . . You really Charley Popcorn?

POPCORN: Forever!

TAM: You ain't shittin me, you ain't signifying, you don't know what I'm talkin about?

(*Soundtrack: sucky fucky noises and music—a simple instrumental version of the "Japanese Sandman"*)

POPCORN: How long's it been since you be sleepin, Mr. Lum?

TAM: Do I sound tired? What're you talkin about?

KENJI: He's been up two days listening to all the tapes he made with the Dancer, gettin ready to meet you, Mr. Popcorn.

POPCORN: Me?

TAM: You! I saw you as a bigger man, man, the way Ovaltine talked about watchin you strip off your shirt, and wash up out of a pan, outside the house. And how his eyes popped out when he was a kid, at your mighty back ripplin with muscles!

POPCORN: Me?

TAM: And the whiplash scars, how they made him cry, and how that made him sure, he'll be a fighter, a fighter down from his soul!

POPCORN: Whiplash never touch *my* back! You're sleepin, young man. Dreamin!

TAM: All right. This is the sheet on you. You're Charley Popcorn, Ovaltine Jack Dancer's Father.

POPCORN: Huh?

TAM: . . . uh lemme finish. Ovaltine when he was a little boy in Mississippi beat up on a white boy, and you told him you all would have to leave that part of the country, and then you told him bout the welts on your back, and gettin whipped. You and the family packed up in a car and Ovaltine remembers you and him pissin by the roadside next to the car with the ladies inside hiding their eyes. You taught him "psychology" by tellin him, no matter how bad he ever got beat, or however he got beat, to always smile, stand up and say, loud, "I did enjoy the fight so very much."

POPCORN: Where you hear all this shit, Mr. Lum?

TAM: From his book, from his mouth, from his aunt, his wife . . .

POPCORN: He wrote it in a BOOK??

TAM: Why, what's wrong?

POPCORN: I ain't nobody's father, especially his'n. I never been no Mississippi, or done none of that.

TAM: You gotta be his father.

POPCORN: I heard o' shotgun weddings but sheeeet . . . I'll show ya.

TAM: Why should he lie? Maybe . . . accidents happen. Maybe it wasn't Mississippi. He was young, got it mixed up. And you, you know, wild oats . . .

POPCORN: Wild oat! I'll show ya. Here! Here now! You look good now. (*Presenting his back*) You see any kind of whip marks? Tell me, now, you see any kind of whiplash or dogbite on me?

TAM: Well, you know . . .

POPCORN: No "well, you know . . ." Just "no," you don't see none of that. (*Dresses, but holds his hardhat in his hands, adjusting insides*) Ovaltine done bullshit you and the whole world, son. If you come all the way here to see Ovaltine's daddy, ha, you come for nothin! Ha! That Ovaltine, just can't leave go of me . . .

TAM: But he *believes* you're his father! He really does.

POPCORN: He believe that, he's crazy!

TAM: Those stories, man! He . . . he drinks his coffee like you do, half milk, half coffee, a spoon of sugar . . .

POPCORN: Yah, I drink it that way, but that don't make me his father. I never made him my son, so how can he make *me* his father? Coffee and condensed milk don't make seed, you understand.

TAM: All he talks about is you.

POPCORN: He do things to make me call him up, that's all. I don't know why. But I never heard of this whiplash and washin up trash.

TAM: Well, why you, man? Why's he think you're his father, where'd all these stories come from? You're his father! You are, man! You are!

POPCORN: That's dreamin, Mr. Lum. Those stories he dreamed, that's not me. That wasn't ever us, even when we were pardners. I always favored him and won't say a word to harm him ever. Let's just say when he started winning, and white people with money and ranches . . . You can't blame anybody if they don't want to live in a room and sometime in the back of an old station wagon no more. But you understand, prizefighting is a business, you gotta be a businessman, you see to be a good prizefighter. I was always a small businessman. A shopkeeper, no tycoon.

TAM: What's this got to do with Ovaltine?

POPCORN: A smart prizefighter, he got to be always thinking ahead, you see. I never knew how to make him champion of the world!

TAM: What'd he do to you?

POPCORN: I won't say nothin against the Dancer. He was champion of the world!

TAM: . . . He couldn't've won the Dupree fight . . .

POPCORN: He . . . that Dupree fight! What he say bout . . . No don't tell me. I'll tell you! He brought me back to train him. The night of the fight . . . I was in Cleveland in a bar, watchin the fight on TV. He fired me, ya see. He'd . . . just say, we'd had words.

TAM: What about? What're you doin to Ovaltine?

POPCORN: About nothin! I'm smalltime, penny ante slick, and that's good enough for me. I was in his way, that's all.

TAM (*standing up animated*): Well, he's sorry, man. He's sorry! He needs you to be his father, can't ya see?

KENJI: Take it easy, man.

TAM: Jerk off! You gotta be his father. Everybody knows you're his father. You can forgive him. You're all the fight he has left! He's an ex-champ, an old forgotten man talkin more about you than his fights.

POPCORN: What kind of shit you blowin at me? You're goofy! Fall down! Fall asleep, young man.

TAM: You can't turn your back on him.

POPCORN: Oh, you are a slick businessman. I see why Ovaltine favors you all right. So he needs a father for this show about him.

TAM: Forget the movie, okay? And listen . . .

POPCORN: Man, you shoulda knowed from those stories, that they was dreams! They was lies! All made up. Bullshit!

TAM: Boys forget, don't you know that?

POPCORN: Grease! Grease! Grease and bullshit!

(TAM *strikes at* POPCORN. POPCORN *easily shoves the punch away*.)

TAM (*to* POPCORN): You gotta be his father.

KENJI (*restraining* TAM): Cool it!

(TAM *elbows* KENJI *in the gut violently and shoves him away*.)

TAM (*to* KENJI): You blew it!

(TAM *confronts* POPCORN *physically*. POPCORN *fends him off*.)

POPCORN: You're so sleepy, you couldn't crack piecrust! Now, stop it, boy. Sit down, damn ya.

TAM: He didn't mean it.

POPCORN: Sit down.

TAM: Never! Fight, man, you can do it. Father of a champion . . .

POPCORN: Why not sit down . . .

TAM: Never, you gotta knock me down.

KENJI: You're gonna fall down, man, come on.

(KENJI *takes* TAM's *shoulders.* TAM *shrugs him off and swings on* POPCORN. POPCORN *steps away from the blow and* TAM *falls on his face, and doesn't move for a beat.* POPCORN *seems embarrassed, and tentatively moves to help* TAM *up but checks himself.* KENJI *is disgusted. He puts his hands in his pockets and looks down on* TAM. TAM *begins to laugh. He hits the floor with his fist and laughs. Rolling over onto his back he says* . . .)

TAM: Never fall. I'm the Chickencoop Chinaman. My punch won't crack an egg, but I'll never fall down. That is why . . . That is why what, Kenji? Why is that?

KENJI: This is why little men love to hear the call of their Chickencoop Chinaman cry, "Buck Buck Bagaw."

TAM: Buck Buck Bagaw. (*Snorts and repeats the call a few times*)

POPCORN: We'll get you home after we close up here, Mr. Lum.

[*Curtain*]

SCENE THREE

(*Scene shifts to Limbo.* TAM *on* POPCORN's *back.*)

TAM: Foong. Wind. I knew the word for wind. I am the only noise of him left. Lawk sur, rain. We said it was Yit, gum yut yit, hot today or gum yut lahng, cold today. Windy, raining, hot or cold today. That's all we talked. Foong chur, lawk gun sur, yit, lahng, gum yut lahng, lawk gun sur, foong chur, gum yut yit . . .

The buck and cluck of this child, your Chickencoop Chinaman gushes furiously. Like sperm. Numerously. Chug and thud, to conceive! With only foong, lawk yur, yit, lahng I had long deep talks with a man I remember to this day, but with all the fine pronouns, synonyms, verbs, adjectives, adverbs, nouns of Barbara's language I'm told I talk good, she left me on my birthday with nothin, it's all talk. In the morning. Chur gun foong. I'd wondered why she'd made my birthday cake early, children. I'd said, "Put on the coffee, okay?" I saw her go out and must've thought she was going to put on the coffee for me. Then later I woke expecting to smell coffee burning, because she hadn't called me. And no one was home . . . My mother called and said she was proud I was taking it so well, and never asked if I was going to fight. IT'S TALK. ALL TALK. NOTHING I CAN'T TALK . . . BUCK BUCK BAGAW. BUCK BUCK BAGAW.

[*Curtain*]

SCENE FOUR

Scene shifts to KENJI'*s apartment. Later that night.*

LEE *is taking the posters off the wall, rolling them up, putting rubber bands around them. She's between taking things apart and putting things together again into something else. She stands tiptoe on a cinder block she's removed from under the table, to remove the tacks holding the tops of the posters to the wall. She repositions the cinder block for each poster.*

Groceries are in various sized bags and cardboard boxes. Piled on the drainboard with the groceries are a Chinese round chopping block and a Chinese cleaver; a sharpening steel; a wok, a wok cover, and utensils (long-handled shaped spatula, spoon, strainer, bamboo scrub brush, extra long bamboo chopsticks); other kitchen utensils; tins of spices; packets, packages, and cans of Chinese and Japanese goods; and a gallon can of peanut oil.

The radio is on, blasting chicken rock and fifties tunes.

TOM, *a very neat, tidy, uptight hip Chinese American. Longish hair, round steel rim glasses. He speaks self-consciously, styling his voice like others style hair. A very cool, deep, intimate voice like an* FM *jock living with his eyes closed to adore his voice. He doesn't walk and gesture so much as move his body from pose to pose. He shies from touches, keeps his hands down, except when moving his hair out of his face. His face is deadpan, except for his premeditated spontaneous keyboard grin that comes up on the offbeat late for introductions and jokes.*

*TOM is warily keeping his distance from LEE, who ignores him.
TOM hangdog goes to the radio and tunes it in. Outside we hear
many footsteps clumping up the stairs. ROBBIE appears out of the
bedroom and runs toward the front door.*

ROBBIE: They're back, Lee . . . I hear 'em.
TOM: Robbie! Hey, Robbie! I didn't know you were here?
LEE: Where else would he be but with me?
TOM: Hey, Robbie, gimme five.
ROBBIE: Hello, Tom. (*Tentatively gives five*)
TOM: You used to call me "Dad."

(*Outside we hear TAM struggling to lift POPCORN and carry him
into the apartment.*)

LEE: You better open the door, Robbie.

(ROBBIE *opens the door.*)

POPCORN: You'll never do it, man.
TAM: We built the fuckin railroad! Moved a whole Sierra Nevada
over . . .
POPCORN: Watch out for my head now. Put me down. You're gonna
fall down and we'll both die!
TAM: Never! Never!
POPCORN: Put me down, put me down! I feel your bones crunchin
up on each other.

(TAM *stumbles in carrying POPCORN.*)

TAM: Never! (TAM *sees TOM, LEE, and ROBBIE staring . . .*) Ah,
Scrooge! I am the ghost of Christmas Past! Ha ha ha ha.
ROBBIE: Hi, Tam!

(TAM *ignores ROBBIE and moves toward TOM and does Alfonso
Bedoya from* Treasure of the Sierra Madre.)

TAM: Say, don't I know zhoo from sawmwheres?
POPCORN: Put me down.
TAM: I don't know how.
POPCORN: I'm gonna throw up. Put me down.

(TAM *spies mattress and staggers toward it. TOM approaches
TAM with his hand out.*)

TOM: Kenji?

(TAM *flops with POPCORN down onto the couch and takes a pack of chewing gum out of his pocket. He unwraps a stick of gum, puts the gum in his mouth, starts chewing, and wads the foil wrapper up in one hand, rolling it around and around nervously.* TOM *offers his hand . . .* TAM *offers the pack of gum . . .*)

TOM: Kenji?

TAM: Gum?

(KENJI *appears in the doorway, wiping his feet. He scans the scene.*)

TOM: Kenji?

TAM: No, oh, you're . . .

TOM: Tom.

TAM: I knew she'd letya in. I wanted her to lock you out.

TOM: You're being very familiar . . .

TAM: That sounds English, Tom. (*Offers pack of gum again*) You chew gum, Tom?

TOM: No, thanks.

TAM: No? Oh. How's *Soul on Rice* coming, Tom?

POPCORN: SOUL ON RICE?

TOM: My book.

TAM: Tom's writing a book. Aren't ya, Tom?

POPCORN: Book? I never heard of a Chinaman writing a book!

TAM (*to* POPCORN): . . . cookbook!

POPCORN: Oh.

TOM: It's not a cookbook.

(TAM *pops another stick of gum in his mouth and adds the foil wrapper to the wad he rolls in one hand.* KENJI *enters.*)

TAM (*cold, through a grin*): I knew it wasn't a cookbook, Tom.

KENJI: I'm Kenji. What's going on here, Lee? What're ya doin?

LEE: I'm fixing this house up.

KENJI: But that's my stuff.

LEE: I said I'm cleaning. I'm tired of living out of trunks. It's not good for Robbie.

KENJI: I thought you were going to Africa.

LEE: Do you want me to leave?

KENJI: I was going to let you stay here til you, you know, were ready to go to Africa.

LEE: Well, I do have a ticket. I can go to Africa anytime. Anyway, the way you moped around here for months, how was I to know you knew how to talk at all? I never knew you were thinking of me. You never told me.

TOM: Excuse me, this must be awkward . . .

KENJI: You must be Tom.

TOM: Go on ahead, brother. This is like watching a movie about me.

LEE: You never told me. Why didn't you tell me, Kenji?

KENJI: I'm the strong silent type.

LEE: That would be cute if someone hadn't said that about Tom.

TOM: Who said that about me, Lee?

TAM: Your mother of course, Tom.

KENJI: Hey, man! Cool it!

LEE: That's right, your mother.

TOM (*to* TAM): And how did you know it was my mother?

TAM: I'm the ghost of Christmas Past, Tom.

TOM: Why do you keep repeating my name like that?

TAM: One question at a time, Tom. Tell me, Tom, seriously, I gotta know . . . (*To* LEE) Excuse me for interrupting . . . (*To* KENJI, *answering a warning look*) I'm seriously interested, okay? Tom, are you really writing a book called *Soul on Rice?*

LEE: He can't stand to be asked questions like that. You can't ask him direct questions like that. Don't look him in the eye.

TOM: It's a book about Chinese-American identity.

TAM: Oh. Thank you, Tom. You're wrong, Lee, he answered that beautifully. You answered that beautifully, Tom.

KENJI: Hey, man! This is my house, okay?

TAM: You talkin to me?

KENJI: Okay?

TAM: Okay.

KENJI: Okay, man, why don't you crash.

TAM: No, man. I wanta rundown slow. I'll just. I won't get in the way. I'll just listen.

LEE: Oh, there'll be plenty to hear.

TAM: Yeah, I can hardly wait.

TOM: Who are you. I'd just like to know. Besides being the ghost of Christmas Past, that is, who are you?

TAM: You don't know who I am?

(TAM *rolls his wad of foil quickly.* KENJI *has seen this before and isn't in the mood for it.*)

KENJI: Hey, no jokes, man. Everyone's tired.

TOM (*to* TAM): No.

TAM: You really don't recognize me?

KENJI: Not now, man.

TOM: No.

TAM: Hold out your hand . . . (TOM *holds out his hand.* TAM *drops the wad of foil gumwrappers in* TOM'*s hand and says* . . .) Here, this silver bullet should tell you who I am!

(TAM *laughs and struts.* LEE *and* POPCORN *laugh.*)

POPCORN: That's a good one!

ROBBIE: I don't get it. What's so funny.

KENJI: It's an old joke, kid. Go to bed.

ROBBIE: You're not my father. You can't tell me what to do.

LEE (*softly, sorry he said that*): Oh, Robbie . . .

KENJI: In my house, you do what I say, okay?

ROBBIE (*to* TAM): Do you like blueberry pancakes?

KENJI: Okay, Robbie?

TOM: You still like pancakes, huh, Robbie?

KENJI: Okay, Robbie?

ROBBIE: I'll make you some in the morning.

TOM: Well, if I'm . . .

ROBBIE: I wasn't talking to you . . .

TAM: You're hustling me, kid. I thought I told you . . .

KENJI: Robbie . . .

LEE: Stop badgering Robbie! Three grown men!

TAM: Well, if you'd stop using him.

ROBBIE: Will you ask Robbie to go to bed, Lee?

TAM: Yeah! Hey, Kenji, let the kid . . .

KENJI (*to* TAM): Later for that!

LEE: Are you angry with me, Kenji?

KENJI: I don't wanta talk in front of the kid. He's a kid.

LEE: Robbie's still my son.

KENJI: Then you and Tom and Robbie all go out in . . .

LEE: . . . by the car and piss in the bushes?

KENJI: . . . out in the hall or somewhere else and talk. This is still my house.

LEE: I didn't think you cared. Have you looked at this place?

KENJI: I don't wanta talk in front of the kid!

LEE: There's nothing to talk about. I told Tom I'm not pregnant.

TOM: That doesn't matter. I want you.

LEE: And we'd live together again.

TOM: Yes.

LEE: You and Robbie and me. Just like before.

TOM: Yes. No! Not like before.

LEE: And we'd have a baby. Another baby.

TOM: I'd like that . . . if we could.

LEE (*turning sharply from* TOM): Mama's boy! Listen to him, Robbie. I wouldn't want another of his children. His mother would only swoop in and take it away from him and me. No, not me. I wouldn't let him or her talk me into that again.

TOM: I think Kenji's right. Not in front of Robbie.

LEE: What do you care? He's not your son!

TAM: Ah! Whose son . . .?

KENJI (*with a warning gesture*): Tam . . .!

TAM: Your house . . .

LEE: Oh, Tam. Be mean and funny! Why aren't you talking. Talk about your movie.

KENJI: Keep Tam out of this. Robbie go to bed.

LEE: You're so bossy all of a sudden. First you get talky, now you're bossy. What'd you do to him, Tam?

KENJI: Let him alone. Robbie, get your ass to bed or get it out of the house.

ROBBIE: You're not my father.

LEE: Robbie, I wish you'd stop saying that please! Let Robbie alone if he's not sleepy. What's happened to Tam? Why isn't he talking?

KENJI: You still here, Robbie?

(KENJI *stares* ROBBIE *down* . . .)

LEE: What's the matter, Tam, cat got your tongue?

TOM: Tam? That your name? Who are you?

LEE: Careful, Tom, Tam isn't what you'd expect.

TOM: What's that supposed to mean? What would I expect of you, Tam?

TAM: He's talkin to me, Kenji, can I talk back?

(ROBBIE *loses the stare-down with* KENJI.)

KENJI: Say, "Goodnight," Robbie.

ROBBIE: Goodnight. (*Exits*)

TOM: 'Night, Robbie.

TAM: G'night, kid.

LEE: Tam just met me today, and he knows me better than you ever did, Tommy.

TOM: Oh, I see it. Lee does this all the time, brother. Games! She's put you through your paces and you don't care. Well, don't be blinded by her white beauty. You're not going to allow a white girl set you against a brother, are you? It's not worth it. I'm tellin you. I was married to Lee, can you dig it?

TAM: I don't see no white girl here. And I'm not hustling none of your ex-wives no matter what color.

LEE: Thanks a lot.

TAM: I'm not bragging, mindya. You're not the only woman I'm not hustling.

TOM: Now who's playing the fool?

TAM: Did I say you were playing the fool? I thought I called you straight out, "fool," fool!

TOM: I'm not prejudiced against Chinese like you. Just between you and me, brother, you have problems.

LEE: Oh, Tom the intellectual!

TAM: You Chinese? You don't talk like a Chinese.

TOM: Listen, you ever looked at yourself? You're willowy.

TAM: What're ya talkin about?

TOM: I'm telling you, for your own good, your peace of mind . . .

TAM: What? You got trouble with the language, Tom? What?

TOM: . . . you better be Chinese because Americans are hungup about homosexuality.

TAM: Huh? Lee, I think his mind just snapped!

TOM: It's true.

TAM: What're ya talking about. What's bein Chinese gotta do with "homosexuality"?

TOM: In American eyes we don't appear as he-men types.

TAM: Oh, we look like queers!

TOM: Yeah.

TAM: But if we read up on Chinese culture, building walls, writin with a brush, talk enough about gunpowder, paper money, Chairman Mao we can fool folks into thinking we're the way we are not because we're queer but because we're Chinese! "Willowy" huh? Me, I'm not going to go round sayin, "I'm not queer, boss, I'm Chinese!" (POPCORN *laughs*.) No wonder she says you're not a man.

TOM: You're prejudiced against Chinese.

TAM: I said Lee says you're not a man!

TOM: You're prejudiced against Chinese!

TAM: Foreigners don't bother me, but ornamental Orientals like you make me sick.

TOM (*interrupting*): I don't know what you're trying to prove, brother. But you'd better face facts. You and me . . . we're both Chinese. Now maybe you don't like being Chinese and you're trying to prove you're something else. I used to be like that. I wondered why we didn't speak up more, then I saw we don't have to. We used to be kicked around, but that's history, brother. Today we have good jobs, good pay, and we're lucky. Americans are proud to say we send more of our kids to college than any other race. We're accepted. We worked hard for it. I've made my peace.

TAM: You sold your baby to be accepted by whites? Now you're at peace? That's too moochie shi-yet!

TOM: I didn't sell my baby.

TAM: Oh?

TOM: My mother didn't like Lee.

TAM: Oh. Why?

TOM: Why? Because she wasn't Chinese.

TAM: Your mother's not Chinese?

TOM: No, *Lee's* not Chinese!

TAM: Tom, you're beautiful. You wanted to be "accepted" by whites so much, you created one to accept you. You didn't know Lee's got a bucket of Chinese blood in her? At least a bucket?

TOM: She's white. Hey, I know! I was married to her. I know Chinese from white.

TAM: Gotcha scared, huh, Tom? How about that funny red in her hair, huh? Peroxide? She just peroxided her hair, Tom. You! Your whole soul, man, has been all washed out, treated, your nerves all taped up and packed away like mummies in the monster movies, man . . .

KENJI: Tam!

TAM (*speaking through*): doin the wicked work of nutty priests. Man, when they dig you up, they're gonna find petrified Cheerios, gobs of Aunt Jemima pancakes, a shiny can of Chun King chopped phooey.

TOM: You're going to call me white. Well, I could call you black!

TAM: Oh, did I turn Tom's feeings? Look at her. Go on up and get a good look, fella, and you tell me who's prejudiced against Chinese. You wanted a white girl so bad, so bad, you turned her white with your magic eyes. You got that anti-Chinaman vision.

TOM: We're wonderful, I can call you "Chinaman" and insult you.

TAM: Do you want to insult me?

TOM: I can call you "Chinese American" and insult you, "Americanized Chinese" and insult you. "Chinese" and insult you, "American" "Chink" "Jap" "Japanese" "White" and insult you, "Black" and insult you. You're angry. I used to be angry like you. I understand, brother. But try to see me.

TAM: What is this talk? *You* should be angry man, pissed off! about this family and Lee foolin you to come out here . . . not this, this smalltalk.

TOM: Let's not lose our heads . . .

TAM: Let's lose our heads! Let's panic, fly off the handle, go off half cocked. Let's act like animals!

KENJI (*taking* TAM *aside violently*): Tam, man, you're making trouble . . .

LEE: What're you doing? I want to hear.

TAM: Lee's terrific . . . putting us all through the hoops, man. The ringmaster!

KENJI: Keep Lee outa your mouth. What're you jumpin all over Tom for? He's a guest in my house.

TAM: What's all this "my house" trash, man? Look, I've eased all the tensions here. Lee's not barking up pregnancy tales. Tom's not pissed off about anything personal. There's no situation! Just a dull party, with smalltalk, man.

KENJI: Why do you talk so god damned much? I used to think it was funny, brave, man, the way you ripped everybody up with your tongue, showin 'em up for clowns and bullshit. Your tongue was fast and flashy with the sounds, man, savin your ass from this and that trouble, making people laugh, man, shooin in the girls . . . I used to know why you were mean and talkin all the time. I don't anymore, and you're still talkin the same crazy talk.

TAM: You were my silent pardner. We used to run together.

KENJI: It's not fun anymore. I never was the runner you were, never as crazy or . . . I don't even know why I admired you. You're vicious now. Vicious! Really . . . all over everybody, calling names . . .

TAM: Is . . . think . . . I've lost my head. I've . . . I must be crazy, huh?

(LEE *laughs*.)

KENJI: I told you it's not funny, now, man. Nobody wants it anymore. You're too old to be badmouthing everything, everything like you do. Nobody's gonna run with that, man.

TAM: Yeah, I'm a loner.

KENJI: You wanta be a loner, you're a loner. You're a mean rogue, somewhere, out there, ya know what I mean?

TAM: Like a mad elephant, blowin his nose alone in the dark.

KENJI: It isn't funny.

LEE: It is funny.

KENJI: I'm tellin ya this. I loved you, man. And if you make a crack about that to Tom I'll take your face off!

TOM: Can't we . . .

KENJI (*to* TOM): Now you be careful o' your mouth!

LEE: Sit down, Kenji, you're scaring me!

TOM: . . . Can't we be friends . . . act like friends at least?

TAM: We should be friends, you know that? Easy, Kenji, I raised my hand before opening my mouth, huh? I know we should be friends. I know that. But I don't want to be your friend.

KENJI: Who you talkin to?

TAM: You have to ask?

KENJI: Who you talkin to?

TAM: Who you got? . . . (TAM *and* KENJI *stare down.*) Why couldn't we have just slapped hands and trotted out old radio shows, dead hit tunes and movies? I don't want to be your friend. I'm tired of you, man. Just one look, and I'm tired of you. I'm tired of everything . . .

KENJI: Tired of talking?

TAM: Really . . . really tired of talking, especially talking. But everytime I stop it's so goddamned awful!

POPCORN: I never been alone with so many Chinese before. Ever! Uh. I never seen so many before without bein in a Chinese restaurant, you know what I mean? I don't mean you be foreigners ha! I know you're American . . . I been listenin, but it's late . . . (*Low nervous chuckle*) I feel like you all lookin at me. You all be lookin at me? Did I say something wrong? I hurt anybody's feelings? Mr. Lum? Mr. Lum, I hurt your feelings?

LEE: Who're you? Everyone's so polite around here.

POPCORN: It's me, Charley Popcorn.

LEE: Oh, I've been hearing about you, you're . . .

POPCORN: No, I ain't no father of no Ovaltine Jack Dancer. I'm just a small businessman minding his own dirty movies.

LEE: Oh, I'm sorry to hear that.

POPCORN: I'm not. Maybe Mr. Lum is though, but he shouldn't be. It's Ovaltine that did him wrong, not me.

TAM: Would you say you're not the Dancer's father on camera, Mr. Popcorn? Hold it! You know what that would do to him?

POPCORN: . . . for one lousy dollar?

TAM: It's my movie, my worry not yours. Be a good movie though, wouldn't it? Make up some hokey connection between faking up a father, not knowing your past, and the killer instinct. But he's an old man now. Trusts me. I've failed all the old men that ever trusted me. Sold 'em out, watched 'em die, lost their names and been . . . been what, Kenji? What've I been for that?

KENJI: Don't ask me.

TAM: . . . You used to be like me, Tom? You've never been like me. You never knew better. I knew better. I must've known better. My whiteness runneth over and blackness . . . but people still send me back to the kitchen, you know what I mean?

TOM: You're oversensitive. You can't be oversensitive.

TAM: You're right. I can't be oversensitive. It's like havin too much taste. But that's me oversensitive. And I like it. I'm not going to dig up the Dancer, mock his birth, make a fool of him just to make a name for myself. That's the way it is with us Chinaman cooks! Dat's the code of the kitchen, children. Anybody hungry? (*Rises to go to kitchen*)

POPCORN: What about the movie, Mr. Lum?

TAM: There won't be a word of fathers in it, Mr. Popcorn. You'll be part of a straight, professional, fight film. I won't need your money, Kenji.

KENJI: Okay.

   (TAM *goes to the kitchen, finds a blue apron among the clutter of packing, and puts it on. He sets to work.*)

LEE: What's wrong? This is all so glum. I don't understand. What about your children, Tam? All your heart. What's happening here?

TAM: I haven't forgotten them. Jonah and Sarah. I'm in the kitchen. A cook. Ovaltine ever fry chicken for ya, Mr. Popcorn?

POPCORN: Yeah, ain't it awful what he do to chickens and grease?

TAM: The Chinatown Kid would've liked to have seen . . . How do I know what he would've liked. You speak Chinese, Tom?

TOM: Some Mandarin.

TAM: No, you couldn't talk to him either. Wrong dialect. It's in the hands, the food. There's conversation for you.

   (TAM *works out with the cleaver on green onions . . . some fast chopping.*)

KENJI: You okay, Tam. You know what you're doing?

TAM: Don't worry about me, Dentist. You got your house, your lab. You're home. I'll cook for ya tonight . . . keep my mouth shut slicin greens and meat, and be gone tomorrow. Roguing like you say.

KENJI: No hard feelings.

TAM: Damn straight I have hard feelings. And I like 'em, they're mine! Thank you. (*Grinning*) Hey, Dentist! I guess you and Lee and the kid'll be moving soon?

KENJI: Yeah, I'm going to be a father.

LEE: What're you talking about?

POPCORN: Sounds like she don't know she's pregnant.

LEE: I heard that, Charley Popcorn. What're you talking about?

POPCORN: You know, I'm having a wonderful time. I really am. Really opens my eyes.

KENJI: I just told Tom we're having a baby.

TOM: Were you talking to me. I didn't know people still did that.

LEE: Are we having a baby?

KENJI: Tell Tom.

TOM: Listen, I didn't mean to walk into any situation.

KENJI: That's right. You think that.

TOM: I'm a good loser.

LEE: Talk to me, Kenji. Not him.

KENJI: I don't know what to talk about, Lee. I don't have the gift of gab . . .

LEE: Sing a song.

KENJI: Lemme talk it.

LEE: Oh, Kenji, talk it then.

KENJI: Somewhere over the rainbow, bluebirds fly . . .

LEE: Not that one. One of your own . . .

KENJI: Gather round the fire boys, and
   I'll tell you how I grew old.
 Seeking Helen Keller's smelly love like
   other men seek gold.
 I rode with the Chickencoop Chinaman, who
   was ornery and cruel,
 Notorious for spinnin a fast mean thread
   offen life's wooden spool.

(*All pat-a-cake up a rhythm, give western hoots and yips and chew cake.*)

KENJI: Listen to this song from the Hollywood Confucius says
   Dostoyevsky West.
 Where the yellow highriders be damned and the slantyeyed
   blind are blessed.

I ride with a killer. I'm a goner. Doomed in my
    lover's quest.
For a long time seeing nothin but sand,
    I've wanted to lose hope.
But I'm STUBBORN, boys, rightly called yellow Blackjap
Kenji,
    Kenji, the Golden Goat.
"Ride," he said. "Ride with me . . ."
    (KENJI, LEE, *and* TOM *freeze, and fade into black. Spot up on*
TAM *in the kitchen.*)

TAM: Ride with me . . . Everything comes sniffin at you in the
kitchen sooner or later, children, grandmaw used to say. In the
kitchen. Always in the kitchen. And listen! Here comes Kenji's
BlackJap song to sniff me up. A long song, from a long time ago,
outa our Oakland.

    Turn off them radios and listen in the kitchen!

    My grandmaw told me, children, how when she was left alone
to roll cigars all by herself, in the Old West when Chinamans was
the only electricity and all the thunder in the mountains . . . in
them awful old days of few mothers, few fathers, and rare
songs . . . she used to leave a light on in the next room, and
listen. And talkin to us—This is true!—sometimes she heard a
train. A Chinaman borne, high steppin Iron Moonhunter, liftin
eagles with its breath! "Listen!" she'd say.

    And we'd listen in the kitchen.

    She was on the air.

    The house she said was like when her father came back from
the granite face and was put in the next room, broken and frostbit
on every finger and toe of him and his ears and nose, from the
granite face, by Chinamans, nobodies' fathers, all night long running stolen horses, yelling for speed, for my grandmaw's ma.
That's the truth!

    Ya hear that cry?

    From China Camp, Jacksonville, Westport, Placerville, a gal-
lop and grandmaw's pa coming home.

    And he died there, in the light of the next room, comfortable,
comforting a little girl rolling counterfeit Spanish cigars.

Now and then, I feel them old days children, the way I feel the prowl of the dogs in the night and the bugs in the leaves and the thunder in the Sierra Nevadas however far they are. The way my grandmother had an ear for trains. Listen, children, I gotta go. Ride Buck Buck Bagaw with me . . . Listen in the kitchen for the Chickencoop Chinaman slowin on home.

[*Curtain*]

Randall "Duk" Kim and Joanna Pang in *The Chickencoop Chinaman*

All photos are by Martha Holmes and are based on performances at the American Place Theatre in New York City.

Merwin Goldsmith, Sab Shimono, Randall "Duk" Kim, and Calvin Jung in *The Chickencoop Chinaman*

Sab Shimono, Randall "Duk" Kim, and Leonard Jackson in *The Chickencoop Chinaman*

Sab Shimono, Sally Kirkland, and Randall "Duk" Kim in *The Chick-encoop Chinaman*

Sab Shimono, Randall "Duk" Kim, Calvin Jung, Leonard Jackson, and Sally Kirkland in *The Chickencoop Chinaman*

The cast of *The Year of the Dragon*: Doug Higgins, Conrad Yama, Pat Suzuki, Randall "Duk" Kim, Tina Chen, Lilah Kan, and Keenan Shimizu

Fred's Chinatown tour in *The Year of the Dragon*

Pat Suzuki and Randall "Duk" Kim in *The Year of the Dragon*

Doug Higgins, Conrad Yama, Tina Chen, Pat Suzuki, Randall "Duk" Kim, and Lilah Kan in *The Year of the Dragon*

Pat Suzuki, Keenan Shimizu, Conrad Yama, Tina Chen, and Lilah Kan in *The Year of the Dragon*

The Year of the Dragon

The Year of the Dragon was first produced at the American Place Theatre, New York City, 22 May 1974:

Directed by Russell Treyz
Associate Director, Julia Miles
Scenery by Leo Yoshimura
Costumes by Susan Hum Buck
Lighting by Victor En Yu Tan

Cast (in order of appearance)

FRED ENG	Randall "Duk" Kim
CHINA MAMA	Lilah Kan
MA (Hyacinth Eng)	Pat Suzuki
SIS (Mattie), "Mama Fu Fu"	Tina Chen
ROSS	Doug Higgins
PA (Wing Eng)	Conrad Yama
JOHNNY ENG	Keenan Shimizu

Characters

FRED ENG, *Chinese American travel agent and tourist guide in his forties.*

CHINA MAMA, *an old Chinese woman. Pa Eng's Chinese wife.*

MA (Hyacinth Eng), *Chinese American. Youngish. In her middle or late fifties. American born and raised. Manically efficient, practical, irrational.*

SIS (Mattie), *"Mama Fu Fu," Chinese American. The married daughter of Ma and Pa Eng. Middle class in dress and manners. Thirtyish.*

ROSS, *Mattie's China-crazy white husband. Aesthetic, supercilious, Mr. Nice Guy.*

PA (Wing Eng), *Chinese in his sixties, dying of a lung disease. A snappy but conservative dresser.*

JOHNNY ENG, *Chinese American in his late teens. A Chinatown street kid.*

Place

An apartment in San Francisco's Chinatown.

Time

Chinese New Year's.

Settings

ACT ONE   SCENE 1: Fred's first last tour of the day. Night.
          SCENE 2: Eng family apartment. Night.
          SCENE 3: Fred's last tour.
          SCENE 4: Eng family apartment. Night.

ACT TWO   SCENE 1: Fred on tour. Night.
          SCENE 2: Eng family apartment. Predawn.
          SCENE 3: Chopsticks. Day.
          SCENE 4: Eng family apartment. Noon.
          SCENE 5: Eng family apartment. Night of the parade.

ACT ONE

SCENE ONE

Fred's first last tour of the day. Night.

FRED:

We'come a Chinatowng, Folks! Ha. Ha. Ha . . . Hoppy New Year!
Fred Eng, "Freddie" of Eng's Chinatown tour'n' travoo.
"We tell Chinatown where to go." Ha ha ha. I'm top guide here.
Allaw week Chinee New Year. Sssssshhh Boom! Muchee muchie
firey crackee! Ha. Ha. Ha . . .
But you're my last tour of the day, folks. And on my last tour of the
day, no hooey. I like to let my hair down. Drop the phony accent.
And be me. Just me.
I figure once a day, I have got to be me.
So tonight, I'm gonna take ya where I eat, "The Imperial Silver Jade
Empress."
Good home cookin and souvenir chopsticks.
I figure you folks who come to me after dark really want to know.
You wanta see the Chinaman albino the color of Spam, and the
sights only Chinatown's topguide can show ya. I might show'em
to ya tonight, folks.
You make me feel good. I like ya. Goong Hay Fot Choy . . .
   (*Leaves cussing under his breath*)
Goddam, motherfucking . . .
                    [*Curtain*]

71

Scene Two

Old Frisco Chinatown apartment. Night. The kitchen is the main center of action. An old gas stove, a newish refrigerator. Kitchen counter. A small TV on top of the refrigerator. A round table with four kitchen chairs. Folding chairs leaning against the wall. A stack of old newspapers against the wall next to the front door. The kitchen is crowded with a neat arrangement of stuff. Kitchen stuff. Sewing stuff. Stuff to be thrown out. A large stockpot simmers on the stove. A coffee can full of sand and painted red is on the shelf before the pictures of the family dead. The can is full of burned out punks. FRED's *desk is set against one wall.*

The bathroom is attached to the kitchen and is another center of action. Magazine rack with magazines and knitting in the bathroom. A clothesline hangs over the bathtub. A man's socks hang, drying on the line. CHINA MAMA *is seated by her luggage. Her hands are folded on her lap. She doesn't move. She sees all, from lumpy peasant fearlessness and dignity.*

MA, SIS, *and* ROSS *come in the front door.* ROSS *and* SIS *carry luggage.*

MA: Well come on in, children and close the door. You can have Fred's room, Sissy. He hardly sleeps home anyway . . . (*Looks at* ROSS *then around the room*)

SIS: Oh, ma, the place hasn't changed a bit. It gives me a chill . . . (*Fixes attention on* CHINA MAMA. CHINA MAMA *stares back.*)

MA: I feel a little dizzy too, now that you mention it. (*Following* SIS's *gaze*) Oh, that! That's pa's problem. Nothing to do with us. Let's just leave it to him . . . But the icebox is new. And I painted the kitchen and the bathroom two years ago. Your two wonderful brothers were too busy allaw time to so much as help me take the lid off the paint cans . . .

SIS (*having glanced into the bathroom*): They still make you do all your knitting in the bathroom, ma?

ROSS: What? Uhhh . . .

MA: Oh, she's only kidding, Ralph. Go on touch anything you want.

SIS (*overlapping*): "Ross," ma.

MA: Oh, I'm no good with names. You might not believe me, Ross, but that's the most comf'able room in the house. It's quiet and has a window and you know when Fred was born he gave me these awful hemmerroids and you and Johnny coming out the way you did dink help . . . and it's so nice just to sit in there and bare my bee tee emm and let the fresh air cirrculake around there, you know . . . oh, what a thing to talk about to newlywed! You know, Rex, my Sissy is a very limited edition. Only twenty Chinese babies born in San Francisco in 1938. So you married what we call a freak of nature, around here . . .

SIS: Ma!

MA: What am I saying? That was just something I must have heard on TV or somewhere, and it just popped out! Sit down you two, you're making me yakity yak I'm so nervous . . .

SIS (*continuing to pace*): No, you sit, ma . . .

MA (*forcing* SIS *into the easy chair*): No, you. You're the guest. Sit! There's your chair. Remember?

SIS: My chair?

MA: It just looks like new cuz I made a new slip cover for it . . .

SIS: Why don't you get some new furniture in here, ma, instead of working so hard . . .?

MA: Don't be silly. I like it. I like to come home and look out the window and it feels like such an old strong house in here when I look out at all the changing out there. So many children and new building and streets that used to go two ways going one ways then the other . . . Now tell me, why did you come *here* for your honeymoon, to this old place? I remember Dappy Dandy took *me* to Yosemite National Park and we drove through a redwood tree on *our* honeymoon, and the cars in those days shake like a bucket of bolts . . . (*Sings a line*) Sing song, sing song, So Hop toy . . . And when he change gears, I change key. "*Alle same like China boy . . .*" Higher you know. Or songs . . . I sang all the way. "*Down in Chinatown there lived a China Boy . . .*"

ROSS: Goong Hay Fot Choy . . . Chinese New Year's . . .

MA: Why dink you tell me and I'm make Fred give you two a honey-
moon to Sydney, Australia, or somewhere new to all of us. It's
Chinese New Year's all over the world, not just here. Shoo!
Sometimes you don't think Sissy . . .

ROSS: Well, Fred wrote us uhh, your husband. Mr. Eng, wants the
whole family together this Chinese New Year's and . . .

MA: Nobody tells me anything til the last minute, around
here . . . and I'm not getting any younger . . .

SIS: This isn't our real honeymoon, ma. We're here to wind up a tour
promoting my cookbook.

ROSS: Let's forget the tour, Mattie. You're back home in the most
famous Chinatown in the world and all of Chinese New Year's to
welcome you . . .

MA: Yes, I love those recipes. They sound like poems out loud. "To 3
gals water in large soup pot add 24 squabs, 3 chickens, 2 guinea
hens, 6 pairs froglegs . . ."

SIS: Oh, ma, please . . .!

ROSS: Mattie, what's wrong, honey?

SIS: I think it's coming to a stop after all this traveling or . . . I
don't know. A honeymoon in Australia . . . I know it's silly, but
all of a sudden I feel like just another yellow girl on the arm of a
Caucasian . . .

MA: If it's anything I said . . .

ROSS (*overlapping*): Well, I . . .

SIS: It's just a shock seeing so many at once. Ross and I must have
looked like part of a special drill team practicing for Saturday's
parade, huh, ma.

MA: The color of somebody's skin donk change the color of their
blood, I always say . . .

SIS: Oh, I'm joking, you two. Don't mind me . . .

MA: You're right, Sissy, before there didn't used to be so many Chinese girls here like nowadays. My grandmother, Ross . . . she
used to tell me she used to come home oh, crying like a sieve cuz
all she saw was blocks and blocks of just men. No girls at all. She
was very lonely. Then she became a madam, if you know what I
mean . . . Coffee or tea, children . . .

SIS: Ma, sit down, and stop . . . (SIS *sits in an easy chair*.)

MA (*having never stopped*): I like calling you children . . . That makes you my son-in-law . . . Ross . . .

SIS *and* ROSS (*overlapping* MA): "Ross."

MA: Dink I say "Ross"?

ROSS: Yes, you did . . .

MA: You know, I've never heard you swear and cuss, Ross.

ROSS: Pardon?

MA: I think you're very nice . . . Oh, Sissy. Do you remember that chair? That's your chair, isn't it. I re-covered it with fabrics I found in grandma's trunk . . .

ROSS: How about that, Mattie . . .?

SIS: I remember sitting here crying. Braiding my hair while you gave Fred a licking after giving me one . . .

MA: Both o' you kids was wongerfuls. I never lay a finger . . .

SIS (*overlapping*): You were crying too, ma. Pa made you whip Fred whenever you whipped me because he was the oldest and should be taking care of me. Ha. And he knew Fred wouldn't hit back at you. I hated it, ma. I'd sit here and pull some hair down in front of my face and try to make something pretty around here . . .

MA: I was going to say, young lady, you and Fred and me gave that chair to your father for Christmas. You picked out the color . . .

SIS: I don't remember that, ma . . .

ROSS (*lying*): Oh, sure you do, honey. You told me, don't you remember? Really, Mrs. Eng, Mattie talks about . . .

MA: See? How could Ross know if you didn't tell him? So how can you say you don't remember? And your brother did too take care of you. Her bawk jer, Ross, *backtalk* got her in so much trouble, whoo . . . the boys . . .

ROSS (*overlapping, under* MA): Maybe you'd like to lie down awhile, honey . . .

SIS: "We'come a Chinatong, forks! Fret Eng. Frettie obba Eng Chinatowng Tooor anna Travooo . . . I'm a Top guy . . .!" Yeah, he took care of me . . . (SIS *drifts her gaze to* CHINA MAMA.)

MA: Why donk he talk like that at home, I want to know . . . Quit looking at her, Sissy. Be polite. Leave her alone . . . Boy, when

Fred comes down the hall . . . It's like a wild animal . . .
Whoops. Listen you two. I have to go out and get some coffee . . .

SIS: Oh, ma, we'll go for ya . . .

MA: No. No. Those boys of mine won't drink plain old Hills Bros.
you can get in any store. They have me go to some out of the way
Italian place and say, "One pound French. One pound American.
Mixed. Ground for filter . . ." And look at their coffeepot! You
ever see such a goofy looking thing? Well, at least they still drink
the same coffee together, I tell pa . . . (*Goes out the front door.
Down the hall, fading out*) Boy what a day. I never heard so many
firecrackers. I don't know how people stand it. I can't believe the
Chinese meant it to be so noisy all the time . . .

ROSS: Well, here we are, honey. You're back home.

SIS: But I'm not sentimental about this place. Fred had a friend who
was. Real sentimental. I sat on his lap in this same chair
. . . "my chair" . . . He had his arm around me. He showed
me the scars of his last knife fight and told me the story of his life
. . .

ROSS: Hmmm . . .

SIS: No, nothing like that . . . I told him Fred was sending me to
college. And he said no matter where I go only this place will ever
have any right to me. Only this Chinatown has the right to judge
me. To kill me. He used to talk like that. Too many movies. The
last stabbing got him. The idiot. Five months in the hospital. I
told him it didn't matter where I was born or what color I
was . . . especially being a Chinese girl. He told me about the
morphine they gave him. The nice nurses. He turned twenty-two
in intensive care, and I was gone. This wasn't my home then. It's
not my home now. My home is with you in Boston, Ross. Nowhere else.

ROSS: If you'd rather stay in a hotel . . .

SIS: No, no. No. You should meet the family and enjoy yourself,
dear. Just bear with me . . .

(*They embrace and take their bags down the hall . . .*)

ROSS: Everything's going to be fine, Mattie. Relax . . .

[*Curtain*]

SCENE THREE

Fred's last tour. Night.

FRED:

We'come a Chinatong, Folks! Ha. Ha. Ha . . .

Goong Hay Fot Choy, Cholly! Ha. Ha. Ha.

Fred Eng. "Freddie!" of Eng's Chinatown Tour'n'Travel.

"We tell Chinatown where to go." Ha. Ha. Ha . . .

I'm topguide here. So buckle up your eyes, folks, and get ready to see!

No more daylight in Chinatown but keep looking.

I'm gonna show ya how to grab sights out of flashing firecrackers and my native multi-colored neon zap. But now you're hungry. Folks.

You wanna know where to go eat in Chinatown, I betcha.

Hard to choose, ain't it. Yessir. I divine with you the same way you divine and fortune tell with the ninety-nine restaurants and suey shops in Chinatown.

Other guides leave you to wander around counting for yourselves. But you're my last tour of the day. So no hooey. No more boo sheet. I'm telling you right now. Only ninety-nine restaurants and suey shops in Chinatown. I eating in every one and can telling you, it's TRUE! What you hear about . . . Cantonese sweet'n'sour goes straight to your scrotum.

Pekingese goo makes you dream in 3-D.

Shanghai hash cures blind drunkenness and raises your I.Q. six points!

And the universal peanut grease

of the Chinatown deepfry lights up

every nerve of your body,

from your vitals to your fingertips

in a glittering interior chandelier

glowing you up so nice and so warm,

Chinatown all you can eat faw two dollar fi'ty cen'

is all you can eat . . .

(Exits, cussing)

Goddamn motherfucking cocksucking sonofabitch . . .

[Curtain]

SCENE FOUR

Eng family apartment. Night. SIS *and* ROSS *are relaxing in the
kitchen.* CHINA MAMA *hasn't moved.*

FRED (*enters by the front door swearing*): Goddamn motherfucking
cocksucking . . . Hey, Sissy, ma meetya at the airport?

SIS (*overlapping, rises and goes to embrace* FRED): Freddie!
. . . You seem so happy!

FRED: Why shouldn't I be, Sis . . . (*Sees* CHINA MAMA)
Who . . . ?

SIS: I think she's been here all day waiting for pa . . .

FRED: Oh . . . Okay . . . I uh . . . Didya tell her you and me
don't talk Chinese?

SIS: How could I? I don't . . . Ha. Ha. Ha.

FRED *and* SIS: I can't believe you're really here!
    (FRED *and* SIS *laugh and embrace.*)

FRED: Ah, my little Mama Fu Fu . . . How bout some of your
brother's sweet'n'sour hoochie koochie . . . ?

SIS: Oh, you're still such a hom sup low . . .

CHINA MAMA: Hom sup low?

FRED (*overlapping*): Sissy's home for her honeymoon, ma. Now
willya believe this can be the last Chinese New Year's in the
world for us? . . .
    (CHINA MAMA *takes her wallet out and looks at photos and* FRED.
    ROSS *enters from hallway, behind* FRED.)

ROSS: Nee ho la mah? (*Shakes hands with* FRED)

FRED: Hi you must be the happy groom. You're . . . Ross . . .

ROSS: Ross . . . Goong hay fot choy.

FRED: "Goong hay fot . . ." (*To* SIS *under his breath*) Why am I
saying this in my own house?

SIS (*cutting* FRED *off*): This is our own medley of prairie animals,
Ross . . .

SIS *and* FRED: YEE AHH AH HA HA HA AHHHH HOOOOOO! Chinatown Jr.
Texas Rangers!

ROSS: I keep telling Mattie I seem to be more Chinese than she
is . . .

FRED: Is this some kind of revenge on the family, Sis? (*Sits and takes off shoes and socks near* CHINA MAMA. *He holds up his feet for her to sniff, after he sniffs*.) Ma, on my very last Chinatown tour, I'm gonna swear at the tourists all day long. The men tourists. Women tourists . . . little children tourists. Tourists yet unborn in the womb of pregnant tourists . . . (*Holds his foot up for* CHINA MAMA *to sniff*)

SIS: Freddie, quit that! Ross, I don't think Fred wants to talk about Chinese things right now . . .

FRED (*overlapping, under* SIS): Didya get me a picture bride for my birthday, ma? You that desperate for me to marry a Chinese girl . . .

SIS: There's no one in the bathroom, Fred . . . Must be jet-lag . . .

ROSS (*overlapping* SIS's *last line*): Oh, don't be silly, Mattie. Why shouldn't he want to talk about his culture with a sincerely interested student of all things Chinese?

FRED: Because I'm a tourist guide and I run forty to sixty of you . . .

SIS (*cutting* FRED *off soothingly*): Not anymore! You're Vice President of Mama Fu Fu's, Inc.!

ROSS: You've been wasting your talent as a tourist guide. She showed me a story you wrote and you . . . you really have a way with local color. Then when she showed me the cookbook she did . . .

FRED: Yeah, Mama Fu Fu! (*Embracing* SIS) The atmospheric patter between the recipes sure makes Chinatown sound like I'd like to live there . . .

SIS: Well, it should. It's just you without the smut.

FRED (*for* MA): Don't ma tell me to always watch my mouth? (*Up and to the bathroom*) Run away with me, ma darling. To Tahiti . . . (*Rattles the knob*)

SIS: Oh, you dirty old hom sup low! I told you she went out for your coffee.

CHINA MAMA: Mutt yeh?

ROSS: Fred, Mama Fu Fu's is expanding.

FRED: We just bought two pounds yesterday . . .

ROSS: We've bought a freezing plant, and big things, Fred . . .

FRED: . . . Big things, yeah . . .

SIS: Ross, let Fred relax enough to swallow his food . . . Are you getting bald, Freddie?

FRED: Yeah, a little on top . . . Yeah, you look good, Sis. No more scaredy cat. No more braces . . .

SIS: Aw, you! You know I never wore braces.

FRED: Oh, that's right! *Johnny* wore braces . . . *You* ran for Miss Chinatown U.S.A. and wore . . . (*indicates falsies*)

SIS (*cutting* FRED *off*): Oh, you would have to remember that. Ah, but Eng's Tour'n'Travel sponsored me.

FRED (*topping* SIS): Ross, in the bathing suit event the officials made all the girls wear falsies! I saved Sissy's and had'em bronzed . . .

SIS: I was very young and at my brother's mercy, Ross . . .

FRED: And I've been saving them for when Sissy got married. The waiting's been worth it, Ross. Now that you're here . . . here I'll get'em . . .

SIS: Fred, everything's ready in Boston.

FRED: That's terrific, Sis.

ROSS: You should see how business has picked up since the cookbook, Fred.

SIS: Remember, Fred. We used to talk about New England. Being in the snow with the family. Living where the seasons change . . .

FRED: Yeah, Chinaman Currier and Ives.

SIS: And they have a country music station on the radio. I checked. And even a small Chinatown to ease your withdrawal pains.

FRED: Tell me bout it, Sis . . .

SIS: Not even the smell is familiar?

FRED: Huh?

SIS: Well, it's nothing like this . . . I was born here, huh?

FRED: Right here in the kitchen. There used to be a door to the hallway then. But I heardya anyway. You're one of the first things I remember . . .

SIS (*overlapping*): Not even the smell is familiar.

FRED: Pa's stopped smoking cigars . . .

SIS: Fred, you're right! . . . I don't smell his cigars.

FRED: That makes two of us. You smell his cigars, Ross? (*To* CHINA MAMA) You? It's unanimous!

SIS: In a few years you can sell your share. Retire and write. Whatever you want . . . even buy a horse and some hay, cowboy . . .

FRED: I'm pushing forty . . . I know what I can write, huh, Ross?

ROSS: I'm having some of those things from your spiels printed up large to hang on the walls of our restaurants and some translated by hand into Chinese calligraphy in Hong Kong. So right next to "A GOOD SON IS NEITHER AN ACTOR NOR A SOLDIER," will be, "PEKINGESE GOO MAKES YOU DREAM IN 3-D." . . . I'd love to put up "CANTONESE SWEET'N'SOUR GOES STRAIGHT TO YOUR SCROTUM!" but ha, ha, ha . . .

FRED: Huh? . . . (*Takes out red envelopes and checks the bills inside each one*) Here are some hoong bow with a fifty dollar bill lie see in 'em. Giv'em to pa when he comes in and wish him happy New Year, okay . . .

ROSS (*overlapping*): ". . . straight to your scrotum!" Ha . . . ha . . .

SIS (*overlapping* FRED): Oh, Fred. You don't have to. We have our own . . .

FRED: Naw, naw, Sis. You hold on to that for . . . I mean, this is my last New Year's in Chinatown, right? And I got odd superstitions. And don't say "Goong hay fot choy," I'm going nuts hearing it all day.

SIS: . . . and saying it all day . . .

FRED (*almost saying it with* SIS): . . . and saying it all day . . . I . . .

ROSS (*taking a hoong bow from* FRED): I respect your wanting to cling to old ways . . .

FRED: Cling to old ways . . . yeah . . . What's going on here, Sis?

SIS (*sneaks a jab at* FRED): Ah ah!

FRED: I don't want any debts or obligations this New Year's, Sis. I wanta be nice to everybody this last time around. I wanta pay for everything. Here's two more to give him when we toast ma and pa before the parade. This New Year's is mine okay? Relax, you're home. (*Code for "I'm in charge here"*)

SIS: Will everyone please stop telling me I'm home. You don't welcome me home and I don't "Gong hay fffffottt . . ."

FRED: No, don't say it! It's a deal! Jeezis! What a hustle, eh, Ross?

SIS: Does that mean you're coming out right after New Year's?

FRED: Stop pouncing, Sis. I can't move till pa's gone. And if we're leavin, we can't just walk out. A lot of our lives're here. I gotta take it all in once and for all. Then I'm gonna take it all off slow. Like a striptease. Then there's pa's funeral . . . finishing up here . . . But you can take Johnny back home with you as security, a down payment, okay? His probation's up in a few days, then he's yours . . . (*Indicates* CHINA MAMA) You know, I've been watching that old woman and I don't think she understands English . . .

SIS (*overlapping*): Probation for what?

FRED: They caught him with a gun. But all the kids are carrying guns today. Only Johnny got caught!

SIS: Oh, Fred . . .

FRED: Nothin to worry about. Too much of ma's artistic temperament. That's all. Seen his snaps? (*Indicates photographs on the wall*)

ROSS: Johnny took these?

FRED: I let him have the back room of the office for a darkroom. The kid's got an eye, huh? He's got the Eng badmouth too, Sissy . . . The tourists love him almost as much as me . . .

ROSS: I'm something of a photographer myself.

FRED: Just watch your cameras in the street . . .

SIS: You couldn't come out sooner?

FRED: You know how I feel, Sis.

SIS: How?

FRED: Don't worry I won't letya stay no matter how you kick and scratch.

SIS: Mama Fu Fu needs ya, cowboy . . .

ROSS: It's easy, Fred . . . Just a matter of writing Mama Fu Fu's syndicated column, patter for her show . . .

FRED: Hey, a show already . . .

ROSS: A new even more "far out" cookbook. The way you write about Chinatown . . .

FRED: I'm going to write the great Chinese American Cookbook, is what. MAMA FU FU'S RICE DEEM SUM right up their ass, cuz no one's gonna read the great Chinese American novel . . .

ROSS: No, that's not what I meant . . . When I . . .

FRED (*having never stopped, goes on*): I'll write a Mama Fu Fu Chinese cookbook that'll drive people crazy! They'll drink soy sauce straight from the bottle. It's gonna be the first Chinese cookbook to win the Pulitzer Prize and make Mama Fu Fu's bigger than Kentucky Fried Chicken.

ROSS (*failing to interrupt; ad lib*): Fred, I know you can write a novel. I sincerely respect your writing ability.

SIS: It's not you, Ross . . .

FRED: Then Chinatown'll fall on its face to us and plate the old gossip about us in solid gold . . .

(MA *enters.*)

FRED: Then Chinatown will be my people, not his, and we'll all be JAPANESE!

MA (*puts coffee down and heads toward the bathroom*): Here you Japanese Kid, put this awful stuff away . . .

FRED: I bought two pounds yesterday, ma, whyn't ya look?

MA (*now in the bathroom, having never stopped talking*): Whoo son, you talking bout what you're gonna do after pa passes away, behind his back, gives me the creeps. You should hear it echo out in the hall! You know I don't think dat's funny. What if pa should hear out in the hall? (*Giggles*) He'll think it's a ghost, "Whooo! Gwai loong ah!"

SIS: Ma, I know it's difficult for you to talk about pa's going to pass . . .

FRED: Run away with me to Bombay, ma.

MA (*having never stopped*): You know between you and me, I didn't really know my son-in-law was a white guy til he was inside the house . . . (*Sings low*) "I'm lonesome but happy, rich but I'm broke, the good Lord knows the reason . . ."

FRED (*overlapping*): I been thinkin about it for ten years, ma. He's really goin. I can feel it. Just think about it, ma . . . (*Sings with* MA) "I'm just a cowpoke."

ROSS: Uhh, Mrs. Eng . . . If I'm a problem, I think we should . . .

MA: At first I thought it was his eyes . . . too far apart. You know what they say about far eyes . . . (*Sings*) "From Cheyenne to Douglas, all the rangers I know . . ." (*Hums*)

FRED: It's not you, Ross. It's okay, ma. We shook hands . . . She thinks I hate all whites, Ross . . . It's not you . . . (*Hums with* MA)

ROSS: I think we should get things out in the open right away. I know your father's dying and so if he's not going to like me, I don't see any reason to . . .

MA (*half overlapping*): But it wasn't his eyes. I just forget what color they are! It was Johnny's friend Horseapple got shot this morning made me forget white guys for awhile . . .

FRED (*between* MA's *lines*): I'm not swearing at him, ma . . . I know about the killing, ma. It's not you Ross. I like him, ma.

MA: I mean Horsepuckie, Johnny's friend, stupid! He looks like a horseapple too!

ROSS: "Horsepuckie?" Eng Sin Nigh?

SIS: Ross . . .

FRED (*overlapping*): Johnny's covered, ma. He's going back to Boston with Ross and Sissy after the parade. (*To* ROSS *and* SIS) Our baby brother, okay? (*To* MA) You don't wanta talk about it. Okay, don't. (*Finishes his rice*) That was good, ma. Whew! Really settles my stomach. . . . Come on out here for a greasy smooch . . . Let's let her see us shakin hands, Ross . . .

MA (*coming out of the bathroom as* FRED *and* ROSS *shake hands*): At last, Fred has a friend closer to his own age.

FRED: What?

MA: Can you believe he eats so much without gaining weight, Ross? Come on, Sissy, help clear the table . . .

ROSS: I . . . I appreciate everything . . . I don't think this is the time for normal Oriental hospitality and restraint. I love her. I married her. You can accept us as part of the family or you can . . .

MA (*comforting* ROSS): The only problem here is Fred's feet smell. Sissy, you pa's too proud to be the first to go, so don't you kids talk like buzzards looking down on the body.

FRED (*kissing* MA, *then beating* ROSS *to the mouth*): It's over, Ross. It was a coded message.

ROSS: I understood! And I agree. We should clear the air before your father comes home. I'm trying to say, I am not totally insensitive to Chinese like most whites are . . . .

FRED: What I said about tourists, wasn't for you, Ross. That's just me, coming home from work . . .

SIS (*overlapping*): Ross, if you want to stay at a hotel that's all right with me. The family will understand. Just say so . . .

FRED: Listen, Ross, it's the rule not the exception for us to marry out white. Out in Boston, I might even marry me a blonde. We're yours. Hell, Chinatown's your private preserve for an endangered species, and you're the park ranger . . . Hey, ma, Ross and me want a drink. One before pa gets home . . . "Break the arrows" . . . "Bury the hatchet."

ROSS: And what I said about your writing. I didn't mean the best you can write is only good for cookbooks. I'm sorry I created that impression . . .

FRED: That's because you haven't been thinking about it. Really. I've been thinking about it . . . I once published a story in a little magazine and gave pa a copy, what the hell . . . "I was a 'writer.' " And he took me out for clams.

SIS: You two must have been getting along.

FRED: Yeah! I thought we were celebrating. I mean, clams! I'm crazy about clams!

SIS: I never did understand how you and pa talk to each other with food.

FRED: Sure, Sis. Food's our only common language. Bok choy and beancake means, "Hello, Freddie." Watercress soup means, "I need a hundred bucks, son." Steamed clams at three in the morning means he was dying (*at* "*dying,*" MA *goes purposefully to the bathroom*) and wanted to tell me where ma couldn't hear us, like she can now . . . (*Whispers*) Want me to slip the *Wall Street Journal* under the door, ma?

MA: I read it already, thank you . . . .

FRED: He asked me to drop out of school and stay with him til he passed. Yeah, I thought we were getting along. Then his friends came by our booth. Chinatown bigshots and pooh bahs, to shake his hand. Pa didn't introduce me. He didn't even see me anymore. They were the fathers of doctors, lawyers, engineers, those puking, fuckfaced monkeyturd . . .

MA: Freddie, your language please . . .

FRED: I'm the first one he goes to when he's dying. I made his tour'n'travel tops in the town, put you through school and set you up, and still he keeps Chinatown from me . . . tells me to get a haircut and put on a tie . . . Ha. Ha. You know, no Chinatown paper has ever mentioned pa has any children at all, much less us, Sissy. And all the time I've been looking for the things in Chinatown that are like me. You're right, Ross, I don't think of myself as a tourist guide all my life. But my own parents won't read a story I write. Then it hit me, "Food's our only common language . . . " Cookbooks! . . . Chinese Cookbooks! Your recipes and my smut knocked me out, Sis. You invented a new literary form. Food pornography . . .

SIS (*laughing*): Oh, you're crazy! It's just spiels and recipes . . .

FRED: And I got an idea for a book of recipes telling the story of a Chinatown family . . . how to make a toasted cheese sandwich without a sound. Then Mama Fu Fu recalls eating it listening to her parents slurp in their quiet little fucks . . .

SIS (*laughing, cutting off* FRED): —Oh, Freddie, for a while I thought you meant it . . .

ROSS (*overlapping*): I think he's serious, Mattie. You're serious, Fred . . .

SIS: No, you just hurt his feelings mentioning his writing like that. It's okay. Fred doesn't bear grudges . . .

FRED (*shuffling papers on his desk*): Look, there's something I wrote on lobster and life around here somewhere.

SIS: I like that . . . "Take a lobster, ladies. Note its color. Not too many spots. They used to laugh at Mama Fu Fu . . ."

FRED (*overlapping*): I've been expecting him to die for so long it's strange to feel it really happening to him. Do ya feel it, ma? I'm already driving up the freeway, thinking of moving, and Johnny's college and Mama Fu Fu. It's gonna be a funny cookbook, Ross. Damn! We'll sell this building. We'll sell the tour'n'travel. We'll take over the world with Mama Fu Fu's, right?

ROSS: A syndicated column.

FRED (*slight overlap*): A syndicated column.

ROSS: Frozen foods.

FRED (*slight overlap*): Frozen food.

ROSS: A syndicated TV show . . .

FRED: Today the world! Tomorrow Chinatown!

(PA *enters through the front door carrying some of* CHINA MAMA's *luggage . . .*)

PA (*cutting* FRED *off*): A Fred! Grown up will you! Too much noises! Scare people inna haw . . . No good!

SIS (*overlapping under* PA): Pa! Dim ah? How's retirement? (*Kisses* PA *on the cheek*)

PA: Huh? Mattie! Good!

SIS (*hands* PA *a red envelope*): Here, Goong Hay Fot Choy . . . (FRED *groans and whimpers*) Oh, I'm sorry, Fred, I forgot . . .

PA (*opens the envelope and sees the fifty dollar bill*): Ohh, really money too! Ha. Ha. Ha. Lie see jow loy. Ha. Ha. Ha. Chinese joke, son! . . . Ah Mattie . . . Seven? Ache? How long . . . ?

SIS: Fourteen years, pa . . .

PA: Wow! Fawteeng!

(ROSS *sticks out a hand with a red envelope in it to* PA.)

PA (*snatching the envelope absentmindedly as he says*): Okay, siddong. Ma, come outta bat'room. I wanna talking allaw body in a room togedders up. When Johnny home, I essplan naysun family aww togedders up. Right now, no argument. Jus' some unnahstaning, okay.

(PA *sits in the easy chair. Takes off his shoes. Pulls slippers out from underneath the chair and slips them on*)

PA: Fred! No radio! You allaw met China Mama? Get acquainted awright?

MA: Do you feel allright, ah-Wing? Come . . .

FRED: What're you talking about?

PA: Jus' some you be patien' anna unnahstanning aw I asking, okay?

Jus' unnahstanning . . . Dis year da Dragon I bringing Fred guh
China Mama from China be allaw my families togedders . . .

MA: China?

FRED: What? Whazzat? What ya do, pa, get me a picture bride . . .

SIS (*cutting* FRED *off*): China Mama? Oh, Fred! Your mother . . .

FRED: What? Wait . . .

MA: Donk worry about it, son, I'll discuss it with pa. Let's wait for
Johnny and we can all eat together . . . (*Sings* Chinese Lullabye *to
herself*)

FRED: What're ya talking about, ma?

ROSS: Nee . . . ho . . . la . . . mah?

PA: Fred, say hello you China Mama . . .

FRED: Pa, you just can't leave this old lady here on the couch . . .
then come home . . . Pa, god dammit! Whyn't the hell . . . you tell
us?

PA: Donk say dammit . . . hell me, I tolling you!

FRED: You could have told us, I mean, what is this? Think of ma
. . .

PA: What I do my businesses. I got ask questions to you faw do what
I do! *Chie!* Craze.

FRED: That's no reason for you to make it hard on everybody . . .
(*All stop*. CHINA MAMA *gives* FRED *lie see* . . .)

SIS: You all right, ma?

MA (*stops singing*): Do people ask you if you're all right every time
you come out of the bathroom, young lady?

CHINA MAMA (*overlapping* MA *and under to Fred*): Ngaw hie nay guh
mah! ("*I'm your mother*.")

FRED: Nay hie a ping gaw uh?

PA: Fred!

SIS (*under*): You asked her if she's an apple . . .

CHINA MAMA: Ngaw hie nay guh mah!

FRED: Yeah, pa. Sis got us a new member of the family.

PA: Dead mouse somewhere? I smell it.

MA: Your son. His feet! (*Gets* PA *a bowl of rice*)

FRED: You blind?

PA: Blin? What you mean "blin"? I talking *nose*. Smell. Whoo! Close

a-door can't you? Anna hepping China Mama dining room
table . . .

MA: You mean I have to cook for her too? Ah-Wing this isn't
China . . .

PA: I'm pa! Nonk you're argue me my house! Ah China Mama
uh . . . hepping you . . .

MA (*walks to the bathroom*): Excuse me, I have to see a man about a
dog . . .

FRED: Ma . . .

(CHINA MAMA *strips off a layer of her outer garments. She wears
a coat, a jacket, several sweaters, vests, blouses . . .* CHINA
MAMA *then heads for the kitchen area to help with dinner.*)

PA (*cutting* MA *off*): Ma! No bat'room willyou?

FRED: . . . Pa! Hold it . . . pa. Whaddaya mean, my China
Mama?

SIS: Fred . . .

FRED: I heard ya, Sis. But I wanta hear it from you, pa. And I wanta
hear it now!

MA: Why donk you set the table before we eat 'stead of argue right
away, son. (*Forcefully moves* CHINA MAMA *away from the kitchen
area*)

PA (*overlapping* MA, *to* FRED): What you wanna know for?

MA: Oh, son, don't just stand there with your mouth wide open like
a fly gonna fly in.

FRED: Pa.

MA: Sing with ma. You know, Russ, alla us used to sing since Armi-
stice Day . . . (MA *shoos* CHINA MAMA *from kitchen area.*) SHOO!
SHOO!

PA: What explain? She young when I leabing China. U.S.A. change
laws an' old lady start come over. Donk I telling you you're Chinese? Surprise!

CHINA MAMA: Nay hie ngaw guh jie . . . ngaw guh bebe . . . (*She
mimes the message that* FRED *is her baby.*)

FRED (*as he's cut off from chanting the song*): "Bebe?" . . .

MA: Okay eat. But you keep her out of my kitchen or . . . Oh, you
fubbernuckie hum buggah . . .!

PA (*to* MA): You're maybe titching her Ning lisses . . .

SIS (*puts an arm around* FRED): Come on, Fred. Sissy's here . . . "Bebe."

FRED: You mean I really am the son of *Flower Drum Song?*

PA (*having never stopped*): . . . and she titchie you Chinese. Good faw bot' o'you at same times. Fred . . . where Johnny?

MA (*overlapping*): I talk Chinese!

FRED: Pa . . .

PA: China Mama IS Chinese!

MA: I'm gonna tie her up if you donk . . .

PA: No arguments me . . . Tire . . .

FRED: You're tired? . . . I'm tired, pa . . .

MA (*overlapping*): Wing, this is my house!

PA: Mah house! Who lib here anybody I say so.

FRED: Pa . . .

MA: Live here? (*Turns and goes to the bathroom*) You tell him, son . . .

FRED: Tell him what?

MA (*goes to the bathroom, slams the door and shouts*): Shit! Piss! Muckle dung!

FRED: Pa, why do you do things like this? Whyn't ya talk to us first. I'm talking mouth, understand? Just give us a little warning . . .

MA: Howzzit go son? Whallallaw mallaw . . .

PA (*overlapping*): Fred, how come Johnny roung Gollen Buddha Gar' when duh shoot duh kit, huh? Too close!

MA (*overlapping, shouting*): Mugger fummer sobba nichie sandwich!

FRED (*normal tone*): Fucking sonofabitch, ma . . . Johnny's covered, pa . . .

MA: What was that?

FRED (*shouting*): Fucking sonofabitch, ma!

MA (*biggest shout of all*): You hear that, pa?

PA (*to* FRED): When you're stop play roung like a kit? Stop swear at ma! Where's dat guy now? I wish you kip an eyes on him. Why nonk you care more da family? Some responsiboos?

(MA *starts humming* Chinese Lullabye [*Sing Song Sing Song So Hop Toy*] *to herself in the bathroom.*)

FRED: Cuz I've been sick and dying for ten years while you were out being Chinatown's topguide . . .

PA (*jokingly*): I nebbah beng tours guy. I dey boss. Responsiboos . . . Ma, what're ya singin for? Alla eat now . . . Fred
. . .! (*Waves Fred to the bathroom door*)

SIS (*overlapping, emerging from under* PA): Oh come on out, ma.
Everybody knows you've been expecting a visit from Dappy
Dandy's China Mama since *before* you were married. Right,
Fred?

FRED: Uhh . . .

SIS: But a visit from your famous and beautiful daughter really floors
ya . . . (*Gives* FRED *a sign*)

FRED: Yeah, ma. You're hurtin Sissy's feelings . . .

SIS: Come out, ma. The family can all eat together . . .

FRED: If ya don't come out I'm gonna kick Ross in the stomach . . .

FRED *and* ROSS (FRED *leading*, ROSS *joining late*): It's not you,
Ross . . . (MA *stops singing.*)

SIS: Come on out and introduce Ross to his father-in-law, ma . . .

(MA *comes out of the bathroom with the clothesline. Stockings
and socks are still attached to the rope. She tries to catch* CHINA
MAMA *with the rope.* FRED *catches* MA.)

FRED: Hey, ma, you okay?

PA (*scolds* MA *for not obeying as soon as she appears*): Haaa! Ngaw
gew nay joe mutt yeah! Nay um joe!

MA: Pa, you haven't met Sissy's . . .

PA: Ma! Donk go no batroom! Will you? Allaw time batroom.

MA: Ah-Wing I think you broke a promise.

(FRED *and* PA *seat* CHINA MAMA. PA *gets* CHINA MAMA *a bowl of
rice and some chopsticks.*)

PA (*to* CHINA MAMA): Nee gaw hie ah Fred ah. Nay guh jie . . . Fred.
("*This is Fred. Your son Fred.*") Cur heck fon jussa likee ngaw
gwai loong! Ha. Ha.

MA: I think your father's head over heels in senility.

PA (*overlapping*): Huh, ma! Jussa likee ngaw gwai loong . . .
uhh . . . a mutt yeah, ha a . . . dragger . . . dragon . . .

MA: I know Chinese! "Ning Ning Nong Nong . . ." Nay guh sir gwai
dow! China Mama!—Wahh! ("*You creep!*")

SIS (*laughs*): Oh ma, pa knows you speak Chinese.

FRED: Hey, pa! Easy on ma, Dappy Dandy, she thinks you're plan-
ning a sex orgy.

SIS (*overlapping*): He was joking. What will Ross think, huh, Ross? (*Nudges Ross*) Pa wasn't making fun of the way you talk . . .

PA (*shakes his head*): Gum dai guh hie mo sahn sing. ("*Such a big boy and no sense.*")

ROSS: The way you speak Chinese . . . Sounds just like Chinese to me.

PA: Bok gwai lo?

FRED: And Ross studied Chinese, ma . . .

MA: Is that right?

PA: Fred! Happy New Year you China Mama.

FRED: What?

PA: Chinese to China Mama! Goong Hay Fot Choy.

FRED: Goong Hay Fot Choy . . . (*Tiptoeing up behind* MA) I'm going to have to tickle ya, ma . . . Come on, Sissy . . . Ma . . .

PA: Ah-Fred! Ngaw gew nay! Over here, doot right!

FRED (*going neither this way nor that*): Hey pa!

PA: Hay for horses! Goong Hay Fot Choy a China Mama!

(FRED *gives up and goes to* CHINA MAMA.)

FRED: Goong hay fot choy.

PA: Awk nay guh ma! ("*Kiss your mother.*")

FRED (*thinking*): "Awk nay guh ma . . . " "Awk . . . nay . . . gum-mah."

MA: Come on, son a big smooch right here. Hubba hubba . . . (*Points to her cheek*)

(FRED *kisses* MA *on the cheek.*)

PA: Kiss your mother over here! (*Indicates* CHINA MAMA)

FRED: Quit kidding, pa. I have a mother. (*To* CHINA MAMA) . . . Uhh. Ngaw . . . yow guh mah over there! . . . (*Reconsiders his Chinese*) Yow gahn mah? Yut gaw mah?

PA: When you grow up? Get responsiboo!

CHINA MAMA (*overlapping* PA *and laying down the law*): Ngaw hai nay guh mah! ("*I am your mother.*")

FRED: "Ngaw hai nay guh mah?"

PA: You my son. You lib my house. Meck my money. Tecking cares you China Mama. Be Chinese now! Jolly time all finish!

MA: Donk forget you're a "Chinese of American descent." Remember Jade Snow Wong, Hiram Fong and Dong Kingman.

FRED (*bright, cheerful*): That's right, ma. Dong . . .

PA: You promised me I'm be happy families when I die? Yes or no?

FRED (*bright, cheerful*): That's right, pa.

SIS: Don't joke, Fred . . .

PA: Jolly time finis! Be Chinese now!

ROSS (*low to* SIS): Maybe we should leave the room.

SIS: Shh!

MA (*overlapping* PA): I don't know how the other American girls stand it. It's filthy. It's dirty. I could never be married to a bigamist.

FRED: Come on, ma. Where's my girl? You coulda been a singer, ma. Play Vegas. And I'd write ya spicy songs to slither out of your throat like barracudas. Come on, we're all gonna eat together, the way you always wanted.

MA: Ah-Sissy, why not presented your husband to you pa? Ah-Wing, you never met Sissy husband before. His name is Russ . . .

SIS: Ross. This is Ross.

ROSS: How do you do . . .

MA: Oh, I'm no good with names. You know what Sissy said when she got home, Wing? "Oh, ma! The place hasn't changed a bit." But it looked different to me as soon as I saw who Sissy married really was, right in . . .

FRED: "Who Sissy married really was " . . . ?

MA: Oh, you know what I mean . . .

ROSS: How do you do Eng Sin Sang . . . or should I say, Ngawk Foo. (*Shakes hands with* PA)

PA (*all smiles and giggling charm in front of a white man*): Oh how're you? Mattie husban? Huh? (*He points from one to the other.*)

MA: I wonder when they gonna have a baby. I tol' her she should have one while we can enjoy it and they should bring it here. We can always make room, you know . . . Huh, grandpa? (MA *tickles* PA.)

PA (*laughs like a kid, then shrugs* MA *off sternly*): Who "gran'pa?"

FRED: What do you think of your son-in-law, pa?

PA (*recoiling from* ROSS; *he suspects a trick*): What do you mean son-in-law, me? Sissy marry?

MA: Yes, isn't that wongerfuls? I think it's wongerfuls!

FRED: You see, Ross, my father has this unique Chinatown condition. He don't understand anything a white man says, even when he seems to. You can say anything to him, and he won't understand. Now if I repeat it word for word, just like you said it in English . . . no translating at all . . . he'll understand me. I'm just telling you that . . .

PA: Him ker hai my guh son-in-law, mo? Yeah? Nee gaw fon gwai lo? (PA *looks at* ROSS, *walks up close and walks around* ROSS *looking him over*.) Hey, how var you? Good? Huh?

ROSS: Nee how boo how?

MA: Will you listen to that?

PA: Whazzat?

ROSS: Nee how boo how?

PA: Huh?

FRED: He said, "Nee how boo how?"

CHINA MAMA (*smiling*): Ah-how! How!

PA: Ho! Man'arin! Good! Poofeck! Poofeck! (*Chuckles*) Talking de Chinee you heap sahbay, huh, son? (*Slaps* ROSS *on the back*) Nee gaw bok gwai lo Jun hai gnaw guh son-in-law? Mo gwong gnaw gah guh, boy.

ROSS: I beg your pardon, sin song.

SIS: He asked Freddie if this white devil is really his son-in-law, and told him not to joke about it.

ROSS: How do you know? You don't speak Chinese.

SIS: Because I don't speak it don't mean I don't understand it when I hear it!

FRED: Welcome home, Sis!

ROSS: But he was looking at me!

FRED: Welcome to Chinatown, Ross! Now that you're in the family we'll give up a few secrets. One of our secrets is how to talk Chinese to a white man so he don't know what you have on your mind.

MA: If Sissy can still understand it to listen to she could talk it if she wanted to. It's probably psychospasmatic . . .

SIS: "Psychosomatic," Ma . . .

MA: Or Psychowhatchamacaller . . . all in the head! You know. I was always taught dat talking two completely incompatible lan-

guages was an asset. (SIS *stifles a laugh*.) Yeah, you can laugh, but
that's exactly what I was told by a teacher . . . Miss Thompson,
she said "Talking two completely incompatible languages is a
great asset."

PA: What're you're talking?

MA: Come on Sissy. Help set the table. Eat! Eat! Hurry. Hurry up!

> (JOHNNY *enters carrying a dancing lion. He is dressed in black
> jeans, black shoes, black tanker jacket, black gloves. He has
> teased his hair into a huge pomp that's high and slick and looks
> like a sperm whale on his head.*)

MA: Donk you say hello anymore? Remember you sissy donk you?

JOHNNY: I knew she was comin . . .

MA: Well say hello to her can't you? And her new husband too.

SIS (*overlapping* MA): Johnny! I hardly recognize you . . .

JOHNNY: Yeah, hello . . . (*Drops lion. Takes off coat*)

PA: Smell Freddie feet! Whoo stinky! Close ah-door!

FRED: My feet are inside not in the hall.

PA: Da win' blow up da smells.

MA: What dat old piece a junks?

ROSS: A dancing lion. The guardian! I've never seen one in a house
before, eh, Johnny?

> (PA *takes some notes and documents written in Chinese out of
> his pocket, puts on his glasses and looks the stuff over*.)

MA: Where ya get dat thing?

JOHNNY: It followed me home from the Golden Buddha Gardens . . .

PA (*overlapping* JOHNNY): Okay! S'allup! No maw jolly time . . .
business . . .

MA (*overlapping* PA): When am I going to get some straight answers
sometimes? You allaw comedians make me a nervous wreck!

PA: Ma!

JOHNNY (*overlapping* MA): All right. It didn't follow me home from
the Golden Buddha Gardens!

PA: Gol'en Buddha Gar'? You stealer dat lie fum my fren resernt?

JOHNNY (*moving on* PA): How come you cross over the other side of
the street every time you see me? How do you think I feel with
my friends, man?

MA (*overlapping*): I'm glad you're home, son.

PA (*overlapping* MA): Friend? Hootlum! Bum! I know! Donk ting I nonk know!

MA (*light overlap*): . . . But why you got to change into doze ol' clo'se fore you come home, huh?

JOHNNY (*overlapping* MA): I'm no bum, pa!

MA: We know you're a good boy, Johnny . . .

FRED (*overlapping* MA, *under*): You keep your chump friends outta the suey shops you use on *my* tours, hear?

JOHNNY: My tours, you mean . . .

FRED: Hey, kid . . . your tours are ruining my business. Tell your friends to eat away from you if they're gonna be shot, and you . . .

PA: What're you're talk?

FRED: . . . get rid of that unsightly bulge . . .

JOHNNY (*having never stopped*): Can I help it if my friends wanta see me make good . . .

PA: More trouble? What nex I asking you?

FRED: Fool! Stealing the lion of a tong from its sacred place inside an expensive Chinatown restaurant means war! Tong war, fool. Just stay away. Your probation's almost up. You don't need trouble.

PA (*ad lib interjections*): What? Tong? You nonk know what you're talking. Tong?

SIS: What?

CHINA MAMA: Mutt yeh?

FRED: We can make good without little Chinamans with guns.

SIS: Oh, Johnny. How can you . . .

FRED: You're going back east to help Sissy out where I don't have to worry boutya.

JOHNNY: Why?

FRED: I didn't raise ya to be a crook or a tourist guide, that's why.

JOHNNY: So what're you? Huh, pa!

PA: When're you two grown up I asking you? Too much noises.

JOHNNY: Pa, me and some friends and Horsepuckie were just standing there, that's all . . .

PA: You mean gangs, no tongs!

FRED: I mean tongs, Pa. Nonk you hear? I talking eyes! Hearing!

SIS: Oh, no, Johnny . . .

JOHNNY: What gangs? We shoot pool. That a gang? Go to movies together, that's all. Play ping pong.

PA: Now Ping Pong gang?

FRED: You mean Ping Pong Tong!

PA: What's 're funny?

JOHNNY (*overlapping*): Them bastards of the Ping Pong Tong are just a bunch of paddle footed (FRED *joins in the line from Johnny's spiel*) . . . fools dancing the willies for a dime!

MA: Oh, you two giving pa a headache!

ROSS: Anything I can do?

FRED: Say hello, Johnny.

JOHNNY (*to* ROSS): Who're you?

ROSS: Ross.

PA: Tong? Whadda you're talking tong for?

ROSS: Your brother-in-law, Johnny.

FRED: Johnny ripped that lion offa the Golden Buddha Gardens today, pa.

ROSS: I like your photographs . . .

JOHNNY: Now we're at war with that lion's tong.

PA: Dat my tong!

FRED *and* JOHNNY (*laughing*): Dat *was* your tong!

FRED: Yeah, kid . . . let's eat . . .

PA (*laughs*): You craze guys . . . (*to* CHINA MAMA) Ker day saw guh! No sahng sing. (*Pokes his finger at his head*)

MA: It's been so long since you boys did anything together around the house . . . Okay, eat, eat, eat . . . Johnny get the bowls . . . Fred, we need another chair . . . don't ya think the boys cheered the place up, pa?

(FRED *moves to get chair sooner or later.*)

JOHNNY (*stands up and goes to the cupboard, turns and sees* FRED *down in the dumps*): Hey, Fred . . .

FRED: You still my girl, ma?

JOHNNY: Fred . . .

FRED: Huh?

JOHNNY (*fork in one hand, chopsticks in another; to* FRED *or* ROSS): Fork or chopsticks?

MA: Come on, Sissy, help, help. You know how . . .
  (SIS *helps set the table* . . .)
FRED (*answering* JOHNNY): Forks! Chopsticks! Gimme lots of every-
  thing tonight. I wanta celebrate the occasion . . .
SIS (*sits down at the table with* ROSS): You really know how to stage a
  welcome for a girl, I must say, Fred . . . You're doing great . . .
FRED: Lemme tellya, one more New Year's like this and I'll fuck a
  one eyed whore in her gooey eye socket . . .
MA: Oh, son, please watch your mouth at the table . . .
FRED: Couldn't live without you telling me to watch my mouth, ma.
  Shows me you're listening . . . (*To* SIS) Remind me to take care of
  that lion tonight, willya?
SIS: What?
ROSS: Can I ask a stupid question . . . Is there really going to be
  trouble. . . ?
SIS: No, Ross, please . . . Ross . . .
ROSS: What are you snapping at me for?
FRED: It's a new patter for the tourists, that's all, Ross . . .
  (*All sit and eat.*)
PA (*picking up his notes*): Okay . . .
ROSS: What is it, Mattie?
SIS: I'm very nervous, Ross. I told you . . .
ROSS (*under*): Why should you be nervous. You're home aren't you?
MA (*touches* PA, *catches* ROSS's *eye*): I told them about our honey-
  moon to Yosemite . . .
PA: Why dey wanna know?
SIS: Pa, you're still so suspicious.
FRED: Yeah, pa, we're on your side remember? Come on, tell us
  about your honeymoon, "Dappy Dandy."
PA: Ah-Sissy!
FRED: Come on, pa . . .
PA: Dey got trees grow onna rote. Yut gaw retwoot tree ho die guh.
  Big. Gotta ho'e in it. Car driving inside anna come out. Honey-
  moon. So what? Nottin . . . Okay . . . now . . . Shh! I wanna talk
  now. Family businesses. (ROSS *laughs*) S'allup! Donk inderupson.
  (*To* MA) Donk go no bat'room. I tolling you right now. Jus' I talk-
  ing. Unnahstan doze?

(MA, SIS, JOHNNY, FRED *grunt, nod, ad lib assent.*)

PA (*to* CHINA MAMA): Ngaw yee gah gong ker day teng, okay? (*"I'm going to tell them now."*) I'm pa. I're be Chinese. I come 'merica year da Ninetee' Torty Fi've. A Fred been a baby . . .

MA (*rising*): Whoops, musta been something I ate . . .

PA (*cutting* MA *off*): Ma! Siddong I tolling you! Okay!

FRED: Come on, ma. Sit on my lap and sing in my ear . . .

PA (*overlapping*): Fred! Too much noises!

CHINA MAMA (*to* JOHNNY *and* FRED): Shhh!

JOHNNY (*under*): Jookcock, Jookcock, Jookcock, Jookcock. (*Slang for "useless Chinese stranger"*)

FRED: Have a heart, willya?

MA (*to* JOHNNY): Johnny, I wish . . .

PA: Okay! No talking! (*Waits for calm*) I'm pa. I been longtime Californ moses obba life. Den I know I die dis year obba Dragons. Tahm chenj. I gotta die Chinese. Cuz I Chinese I gotta bring China Mama over and die in Chinese families wit' Fred . . .

MA (*starts talking low, evenly, almost cheerfully, at* PA's *first mention of death; she avoids* PA's *eyes; she seems to be addressing her children, but more and more the drift of her speech seems to favor* ROSS): I coulda been deported just for marrying your pa. The law scared me to death but it make you pa so thrilling to me. I'm American of Chinese descent . . .

   (PA *consults notes. Looks up, silently rages at* MA. *He and* CHINA MAMA *exchange looks.*)

MA (*having never stopped plods on, doomed to be serious*): . . . I always told you to be proud to be a blend of the best of the East and the best of the West. (*To* ROSS) I'm not the same, but I'm as American as you, you know. And I broke the law. That's not American I know . . .

PA: No inda Russians!

FRED: Huh?

PA: No in-duh-rup-sons!

MA (*turns to* PA *and her voice and temper take aim and come slouching out, and get on him*): But I was crazy bout you my Dappy Dandy. Our love was a U. S. Federal crime and I was only fifteen. We was accomplices being married like folks hijack a jet plane.

(*To* ROSS) That's American isn't it?

PA: I're not finis', ma . . . ma . . . siddong!

FRED (*overlapping* PA): Run away with me ma, hubba hubba.

SIS: Freddie!

JOHNNY: Yum! Yum! Hubba hubba, ma.

FRED: What?

SIS: Johnny!

MA (*having never stopped, looses against* PA; *she has picked up the rope*): The law! The law! The same scary law said she can't come over. She can't come over. That's the law. She can't come over. You promised me. Now she's over! And where's any law scaring her to death like it do to me? That is not fair! But all right! You don't wanna be fair! (*Throws the rope over* CHINA MAMA *and ties her up*) I'll be fair. Ah-Wing, I'll be fair . . .

FRED (*up and after* MA): Last night I dreamed you were naked, ma. Your body was so . . .

JOHNNY (*overlapping* FRED): I dreamed I took off all your clothes by myself, ma . . .

MA: Watch your mouth, young man . . .

FRED (*taking* MA *aside to sit*): Tell me something, ma . . .

SIS (*cutting* FRED *off*): Fred! That's enough! Johnny!

PA (*beats* SIS *to the mouth*): Sissy!

FRED: Hey, ma, where's my girl?

MA: Why're you gotta talk to me that way, son?

PA: A Fred! Dis're be businesses! Serious' (*Waits for mood to settle*) Fred, dis you mama. In China we marry.

MA: A Wing, you know Fred is my son. Dink he gimme hemmerroids when he was born? I haven't been able to go . . . see a man about . . .

PA: Ma!

MA: Wing! You promised me! Oh, Fred! You don't know what you're talking about.

FRED: Huh?

PA (*indicates* CHINA MAMA): Fred! Dis you mama. Sissy, Johnny, you mama over dere . . . (*Indicates* MA)

JOHNNY (*under*): Hi, ma!

PA (*having never stopped goes on*): Ma . . . Johnny. You nonk like a

China Mama libbing here, okay. No probum. We move out nudder places. Okay. Dat what you want, ma? Okay. Fred an' China
Mama . . . me lib out nudder places. I stew teck caring you, nebbah mind what. Pa fix up. You always home in Chinatown somewhere. I pass away, pa sociations nebbuh let you too col'. Nebbuh
you starving. Johnny should working anyway. Get responsiboos.
No maw da hootlum. You know what I men, donk you? Get haircut. Working more fo' Fred . . .

JOHNNY (*under*): Yeah, Fred!

FRED: Not me. Johnny's goin to college.

PA: Johnny be here when I die!

FRED: All right, he'll be here. But he's not goin to run no more tours
with me. And I'm not gonna move out on ma.

PA: You lib my house. You eat my foods. You wearing my clothings.
You my son. Do like I saying you do.

FRED: Johnny doesn't work in Chinatown and I don't move out on
ma.

PA: You Chinese! Yes and no. China Mama, you mama!

FRED: No! No, pa, you know what I am. And you know why I've
stayed here. But you just said ma and Johnny don't have to stay.
So, ma why . . .

PA: No talking! I finis' first.

FRED: Pa, no shit, I'm telling ya . . . (*Crosses to* PA)

MA (*chopping* FRED *off*): Don't interrupt your father, son.

FRED: What're ya saying, ma?

PA: Ma! Too much inderupsons!

SIS (*covering* PA): Will you stop it! (*To* MA): Why do you let them do
it, ma?

PA: Too much inn dee rup . . . sss

SIS (*having never stopped*): Ma's babied and pampered you all her
life. I watched her cry her eyes out while she beat Fred with
wooden coat hangers til they broke. For you!

FRED (*ad lib under* SIS): Drop it, Sis.

SIS (*having never stopped*): And instead of ever asking where you'd
been out to, she'd stay up making your favorite apple pies . . .

PA: Ha. Ha. My favor' appoo pie, huh?

MA: Well, I do make'em better than Fong Fong's . . .

SIS: She'd be up making pies for the freezer and baking til after you'd come home and gone to bed with not so much as a word to her . . .

MA: Oh, he's just the strong silent type!

SIS: Listen! She still makes the same excuses for you, pa. You just can't tell her . . . Can't you see what you've done pa? Just listen . . .

PA (*cutting her off with a hunk of ice*): Who you? You! Talk me like dat my house?

SIS: I'm your only daughter.

PA: What dat you say? No daughter talk inder-upson pa . . .

SIS: I'm not afraid of you, pa . . .

MA (*cutting SIS off*): Let's keep the family all together, ah-Wing. I don't want you to move out on me. Sissy's right! I have to stay here . . .

SIS: You don't! Think of something new, ma. We have some money now. A good business we enjoy . . . a house . . . Forget China-town and let's just be people!

PA (*cutting SIS off*): Whatya talking?

MA: We don't need a house, Sissy . . .

SIS: I'm talking about being practical with what we've worked for . . . and our talents . . .

MA: Oh, "practical" sometimes you don't even have common sense.

SIS: Ross didn't marry one of his own and nobody cares, but you make me feel like . . . Fred! Tell ma she doesn't have to stay here . . .

PA: Dat what you want? Okay, you business. China Mama, Fred, me stay here. Dis house okay for me. Ma'n'Johnny wanna go, okay . . .

JOHNNY: Hey, pa . . .

SIS: Well, Fred . . . ?

PA: Dis some more you big idea, huh, son? What nex' I asking you?

MA: Let's keep the family together, Ah-Wing. Fred. I want to stay home with pa . . .

SIS: Pa will listen if *you* ask him, ma.

MA: Please, allaw you! Stop shouting at me! Listen to you pa!

PA: Okay . . .

MA: If I was the first to go. You know I wish I was the first to go, pa. Right this minute . . .

PA: Aww, ma . . .

FRED: Ma . . .

MA: Den my ghos' come back and I'll *pinch* your toes!
(PA *giggles*.)

SIS: Pa, I didn't mean it when I said . . .

MA: Pa knows, Sissy, so . . . When I go . . . I know I'd like to be in the same house with all my family. Everybody I ever knew. Even the ones that has passed away. Like Toulouse Lautrec in that *Moulin Rouge* movie. I miss them all so. The live ones wouldn't be enough. Since naturally they're the only ones I could see, all the live ones would have to be there . . . not one missing . . . or I'd be so frightened, my strong, silent Dappy Dandy . . .

FRED: I think I saw that movie last night in that redhead's room, ma. She was licking my . . .

JOHNNY *and* SIS: Fred!

SIS: Why? You're like some monster! What's happened to you?

FRED: Everything's okay. Nothing's changed, Sis.

PA: Dat min you stay? . . . A Fred? Okay?

MA: You just like dat Benson Fong in *Flower Drum Song* cough alla time when you nervous agitations.

PA: Okay. A Fred. Okay. (*Mumbles into* CHINA MAMA*'s ear. Looks up and glances at his notes*) I finis' now. Allaw my kit doy, A Fred, A Sissy, A Johnny . . . come tell pa goong hay fot choy from last new year before deaths. Meck me happy. Pa hoping him meck you happys be da Mayor obba Chinatowng dis years. Meck da spitch onna radio from parade! (*Is left standing with his arms out wide and grinning an instant*)

FRED (*low, lagging, sluggish*): Oh. "Mayor obba Chinatowng." Congratulations, pa.

SIS (*lagging*): Oh, pa, that's great!

JOHNNY (*up*): Wow! Mayor! Goong Hay! Goong Hay!

ROSS (*rising to shake hands slowly*): Congratulations!

PA (*cutting* ROSS *off*): I nock finis' yet. One more ting. I tolling you!
. . . Pa! (*A big grin on his face and his arms outspread*)

(*All cheer but* FRED. *All but* FRED *go to* PA, *pat him on back, hug, kiss . . . Ad lib congratulations.*)

MA (*speaking during congratulations; sidles up to* PA *and embraces him*): Oh, tell me you're still nuts about me my Dappy Dandy . . .

SIS (*faking shock*): Ma! I'm shocked! Right here in front of everybody!

MA: A hippie whistled at me today, A Wing.

PA (*to* ROSS): . . . Mebbe you're (*makes writing gestures over some notes he holds in his hand*) Fix up Englis' faw my New Year spitch, okay?

ROSS: I'll be glad to. Ngaw sick wooey gong Joong Gawk wah.

(PA *looks at the notes again before handing them to* ROSS.)

PA: Huh?

JOHNNY: He said, "Ngaw sick wooie gong joong gawk wah."

FRED: Jeezis!

PA (*to* ROSS): See dis? You know how write joke? . . . You read, dat.

SIS (*overlapping, under* PA): Fred, can I talk to you?

(FRED's *attention goes to* PA *and* ROSS.)

JOHNNY: I'll helpya out and pa can tell me how to run the tour'n travel til I . . .

FRED: How bout me, pa? I . . .

PA (*to* ROSS): Spesul I be funny dere. Okay? More good. Peebah remember better when a joke. Okay . . .

FRED: I used to be an English major.

PA (*rises and shoves the notes to Ross and prevents* FRED *from getting them*): What you know? No college graduation? Him Merican. Know da Engliss poofeck. You Chinese! Ma, you tichin China Mama talk some Engliss . . . not too much . . . jussa nuff da's all . . . (*To* CHINA MAMA) Ngaw gaew ker gow nay ying mun. ("*I told her to teach you English.*")

JOHNNY (*overlapping, over* PA): Fred, lemme try it.

CHINA MAMA: Ho. Ho. Ngaw gow ker gong hong wah.

MA: I know how to talk Chinese!

PA: China Mama be real Chinese! (*To* FRED *and* JOHNNY) When you two grown up, huh? . . . How! My sociation lion, huh? (*Picks up the lion and fusses with it*)

ROSS (*to* SIS): Do you think a Charlie Chan joke at the parade . . .

SIS (*cuts* ROSS *off*): Oh, Shhh!

PA: I teach allabody else. Nawbolly dance dat lahn such a like lifes. So really it look . . . (*Fusses and plays with the lion. Works its eyelids, ears, mouth; starts dancing*)

SIS: Fred?

FRED: Not now, Sis . . . Lemme think . . . Hey, Pa! (*Starts clapping time*) Show biz is in my veins!

MA: Oh, son . . .!

(*All beat time on whatever's handy. PA starts dancing in earnest. Lion drums and gongs from outside beat and pound into the room. JOHNNY becomes the lion's tail.*)

MA: What're you tink you're doing? You know you too ol' for dat!

(PA *dancing on. All are dancing or beating time.* CHINA MAMA *joins* FRED *clapping time.*)

FRED: Sis, Madame Chiang Kai-Shek's driving me nuts! I felt like puking, then I felt like laughing, now I have a hardon. Ha. Ha. Ha.

SIS: Oh, you hom sup low!

CHINA MAMA: Hom sup low?

MA: Ah-Wing!

(ROSS *stops eating, gets out from behind the table, moves around* SIS, *and jumps onto the kitchen floor in front of* PA. *With his arms up and crookedly pointing at* PA, *and with his fingers tensed out as if he were casting a spell, he shouts above the noise and dancing . . .*)

ROSS: "The father laughs in wonderment at every little thing his child does. As a sign of his WEALTH and revealed his liking." I like your family Mattie.

JOHNNY (*shouting*): I like to punch you in the mouth.

FRED (*shouting*): He hates white people. Lo fan . . . hates em.

ROSS (*shouting*): And you don't?

MA (*shouting*): Ah-Wing, you're looking like a fool of yourself! (*Her fear gives way to a fit of laughing at him and pointing at him, which makes* PA *laugh, which makes* MA *laugh harder.*)

FRED (*shouting*): They give me a living. I'm God's gift to sluts!

ROSS (*shouting*): What do you mean by that?

SIS (*shouting*): Don't let him getya started.

ROSS (*shouting*): What?

SIS (*shouting*): Just don't talk to him. (*Points at Fred*)

PA (*shouting*): Kip it up! Whooo! (*Dancing hard*)

(PA *begins to weaken and slow. He coughs.*)

MA (*goes into the bathroom*): Whoops! Whoops! Gotta see a man about a horse.

(PA *collapses. His breathing turns to wheezing that turns into a noisy lush sound of bubbling boiling rubber mixed with coughs.* FRED *goes to* PA, *helps him over to the bathroom.*)

SIS: What is it?

FRED: Nothing. Get the door, okay? Ma, can you come out so we can come in?

(MA *lights a stick of incense . . . one of many stuck in a coffee can full of sand on the windowsill. She opens the window, and the sound of exploding firecrackers outside becomes louder. She comes out of the bathroom with another burning stick of incense.* FRED *and* PA *enter the bathroom.* MA *takes the stick of incense to the shrine on a high shelf. The shrine is a one-pound coffee can painted red and filled with sand; on two arms of tubing out from the coffee can and then straight up are two tunafish cans painted red and filled with sand. In the sand of all the cans are the stumps of burned out punk.* MA *puts the stick of incense punk in the sand of the shrine. Behind the shrine are family portraits of individuals and groups, pictures of various sizes in different frames from various periods.*)

ROSS: Should we call a doctor?

SIS: There's a number on the deskpad. (*Indicates area around the phone*)

(ROSS *moves a hand to pick up the phone.* JOHNNY *is up and takes the phone from* ROSS *and hangs up; he begins the return trip to his chair.*)

ROSS: Is your father all right, you think?

JOHNNY: Don't use the phone in this house.

(ROSS *begins to speak but* SIS *motions him to cool it.* ROSS *returns to the table and works on* PA's *speech.* JOHNNY *gets a dustpan and hands it to* MA. *He tucks in his shirt, combs his hair,*

turns the TV on. Checks his watch and flips the channel selector.
MA *meanwhile drifts into singing* Chinese Lullabye *to her-*
self . . . CHINA MAMA *shakes her head and walks about the*
room.)
MA *(sweeping the floor):*

> Sing song, sing song, so hop toy
> Allee same like China Boy.
> But he sellee girl with joy,
> Pity poor Ming Toy . . .

(SIS *and* ROSS *watch and listen to everything.* PA's *attack sub-*
sides under MA's *song.* FRED *lights another stick of punk and*
sticks it in the can of sand.)
PA: What're you do?
FRED: Lightin up a punk to cover the smell.
PA: Dat's you ma pretty smell, son. Meck da flowah grow.
FRED: Not the shit. The blood. Smells like dead chickens.
PA: Huh?
FRED: The smell doesn't go away anymore.
PA *(spits one last time into the sink, runs water, catches his breath):*
Okay . . . a son. He'pping me over to crap now.
(FRED *helps* PA *to toilet.* PA *drops his pants and sits on the toi-*
let.)
PA: Mayor obba Chinatowng . . . *(Grunts and screws up his face*
as he shits)
FRED: Old man, you'll never make that speech . . .
PA: Nutting talk about now. I tolling allabody I die, nutting talk.
Happy! *(Grunting out a long shit, he rehearses his speech.)* "Misser massa-da sermonies . . . *(And continues shitting)*
FRED: The thrill will killya . . .
PA: Misser dah Mayors anna you wifes . . . Destin-gish Presden'
obba 'sociationses anna all you wifes too . . . *(Begins shoving*
out the world's longest turd) Misser Police Chief anny lady anner
gennehmans . . . Fois . . . Happy-New-Year. Goong-hay-fot-
choy . . . " *(Finishes the world's longest turd and sighs)* I wanna
you fix up some Englis my spitch faw I gib back, Sissy husban' . . .

FRED: Huh?

PA: No good he ting I Englis too stupid. Better he ting Sissy pa be somebody spesul . . . like ma ting obba me. Okay?

FRED: Okay what?

PA: Write faw me den I gib a Sissy husband . . .

FRED: I'll think about it . . .

PA: What ting about? You my son, yes or no?

FRED: Yes, okay . . .

PA: Okay . . .

FRED: The least you can do is talk to me like a man and quit clowning . . . (*He unrolls some toilet paper and folds it over into a pad.*)

PA: When you grow up fois' meck someting yourself? Den I . . .

FRED (*handing* PA *the pad of toilet paper*): Here wipe your own ass for a change. (*Turns to leave then stops*) Pa, why do you have to make things so hard on us for?

PA: Nobody say life's easy.

FRED: You're making it hard, pa.

PA: What're you do when I pass away? You . . .

FRED (*cutting* PA *off*): You wanna die Chinese, whyn't you go to China to die?

PA: What're you mad for? I die you get mad? Ha! What China? My house dis! Where I working? Dis my home. You my son. You ting about dat? I dead, what you do? Play wit' Johnny an' ma alla time? Too much fun?

FRED: I'm moving the . . .

PA: Whazzat? (*Coughs*)

FRED: I'm thinking of moving the family after you pass.

PA: Promise me Chinatowng always you home.

FRED: Pa, I said, I'm thinking . . .

PA: How you move? How earning living. No college graduation. I wanta know ma and Johnny and China Mama and Sissy care for after I die. Can you do dat, huh?

FRED: You know I'll always have a home for'em, pa.

PA: You home here. Where you always teck care of cuz you my son . . . No prob'um . . .

FRED: Even China Mama. I'll take care of'em. I've been putting my share of the profits into Sissy's business . . .

PA: How you teck care, huh? You no self-improvement, no higher education?

FRED Me and Sis got Mama Fu Fu's and uh . . .

PA: I sneaking you over Merican what for? Some flop.

FRED (*having never stopped*): "No dockah no lawyah." Listen, pa. We wrote a cookbook that's a hit and . . .

PA: Cookbook? Sissy go colleges what happening. Bok gwai low! And no more blood. No more Chinese babies born in a family. No Merican Chinese babies, nutting doing and flop. You! Born in China. Loud baby! Ma raising you Merican. I die and you a cookbook?

FRED: I'm trying to talk to ya, pa. I'd like to have a talk. I want you to know you insulted me when you didn't tell me you were bringing China Mama . . .

PA: What talk? I ask you promise me Chinatowng always you home. Donk you hear?

FRED: Pa, I think you owe me a talk!

PA: You home here. Where you always teck care of cuz you my son! No more talk.

FRED: Pa, I think you owe me a favor!

PA: You older. Goin craze. Too much noises like a wil' annie moo . . .

FRED: I gave up something for coming in here with you every night. I feel I'm not as good . . .

PA: Goot for what? You come home. Who ting you a man? Likee some spoil kit. Dorty ol' clothe. Dorty hair . . . Jus' playing inna college. What good for? You gimme you story. Torty year ol' you come home, what you show for it? T'ree stupi' page in a cheap book?

FRED: Whaddaya know about it. You can't even read English. How long you been here? Jookcock . . .

PA: I gib you da travoo agen's meck you some responsiboo what happening? You run around like doze tour guy you hire. No good for Chinese peeber.

FRED: I've been here all but two years of my life. But you and everybody always tell me I'm nothing like the people here . . .

PA: Gib up all you craze idea . . .

FRED: Blabbing at the tourists is as close to writing I can do without Chinatown hating me. I wantya to know what I . . .

PA: You never be famous. Wasting time! Stay Chinatown. I be famous. You my son obba Chinatown famous pa . . . I know you care for. Out dere, you donk no can teck caring even you'self, so better you gib up allaw you idea . . .

FRED: You really think I'm a flop. I thought it was some kind of joke between us, but you really think I'm a flop.

PA: You flop all right.

FRED: Ma and Sis think I'm a genius. Johnny don't think I'm that smart, but they all think I gave up something for coming in here with you every night for the last ten years! And you think I'm a flop! Do you understand, old man? (*Slowly*) Ma and Sis. They think I . . .

PA: Will you s'allup will you? Chie!

SIS (*to* JOHNNY): Do you hear them in there?

PA (*having never stopped*): Dis China New Years! Clean house! My birthday! Badlucks!

FRED: Clean house? Damn ya, I'll clean this house out!

PA: Haa! Nay gick say ngaw ah! ("*Haa! You'll bug me to death!*") Donk Damnya me, I tolling you!

FRED: You wanna clean house for New Year's? Okay, no problem . . . No problem . . .

SIS: Out there we'll be able to forget we're Chinamen, just forget all this and just be people and Fred will write again. Maybe he won't publish, but here he doesn't even . . .

JOHNNY (*cutting* SIS *off, low, innocent, and cold*): You have to forget you're a Chinatown girl to be just people, Sis?

PA (*to* FRED): Donk worry my house clean. Mah house. My business!

FRED: Your house? Your business?

SIS: Well, do you hear them? How can you . . .

FRED: You really think you pay the bills? . . . Okay . . .

JOHNNY (*getting away from* SIS, *fast*): "Fred," the "Bathroom," "Bum": that's all I hear around here . . .

FRED: Okay. Well the flop's getting outta your *house* and givin you back your *business*, right now!

JOHNNY: He never asks me to go in there. Always Fred. An' if Fred's not here, he waits.

FRED (*overlapping lightly*): You're going to die alone here with China Mama . . .

JOHNNY (*up and to the bathroom door*): Fred!

PA: Why you're talk so tough wit me for? Huh?

FRED: No other kind of talk gets through to ya. And the time for your skinnying out is past, you . . .

SIS: Fred! What are you doing?

PA: I knew you allaw time hate me. Why?

FRED: No more trick questions . . . I'm all over hatin ya. You thinking I hate ya didn't hurt me a bit . . . It's just gone, pa, and your forty year old flop's going after it. I'm gonna watch you lead my tour tonight, pa! I'm gonna . . .

SIS (*cutting* FRED *off*): Fred, come out of there . . .

PA (*overlapping* SIS): Be useful or lemme lonely finis off my crap, huh?

FRED: Did ya understand me? Want me to try it in Chinese?

SIS (*rapping on the door*): Fred, come out of there a minute.

PA: Aw, you grow up fois', huh?

(*Fred comes out of the bathroom.*)

JOHNNY: What're you doin in there? I want ya to know I really love being your brother.

ROSS (*overlapping* JOHNNY, *under*): Incense is lit on special occasions before pictures of the dead, did you know that, Mattie?

FRED (*nonstop*): Everybody one vote. All in favor of leaving right after New Year's raise your hand. Majority rules, meeting's adjourned, start packing . . .

ROSS (*low*): On anniversaries of the family dead, right, Mattie?

SIS (*low*): I think so.

JOHNNY (*to* ROSS, *cutting off* FRED): Way! A bok gwai lo!

ROSS: Huh?

JOHNNY: Why you pretendin to talk about Chinese stuff when you're really listening in on us?

ROSS: I'd like to know what scent you're burning now. It's familiar, but I can't . . .

JOHNNY: It's Jell-O.

ROSS (*sniffs*): I think it is Jell-O.

MA: Oh, don't believe anything doze lugs say.

JOHNNY: Sweep the floor, ma.

SIS: "Sweep the floor, ma"?

ROSS (*overlapping* SIS): "Sweep the floor, ma"? I've never seen anybody treat their parents . . .

FRED: It's just that we have so many parents, Ross.

ROSS (*to* JOHNNY): I want to like you, I'm trying to like you . . . If you're coming to Boston with Sissy and . . .

JOHNNY: Who are you comin into my home tellin me you want to like me?

FRED: Why don't you take Ross and Sis out, get some ice cream and show'em Grant Avenue, ma, before it gets too full of tourists.

SIS: Fred . . .

FRED (*having never stopped, goes on*): There are twenty-five thousand tourists out there right now and more every day until the parade . . . You'll look out that window and see so many white people's faces and hair, it'll look like a sparkling gravel path and I feel like I can go take a walk on bok gwai's faces . . . it'll be like making wine . . .

MA: Oh, Peter Lorre, son. Do Liberace now . . .

SIS: Fred, this isn't funny . . .

ROSS (*cutting* SIS *off*): What is this 'bok gwai" you keep calling me?

FRED: You know the word, "Honkie"! Huh? "Gringo"? What kind of people call you "Anglo," "Ofay," "Goy," "Gavacho," "Gray," "Haole"? . . . Aw, the hell with all of ya . . . (*Out the door*)

SIS: Fred!

PA: A Fred. Okay . . .

[*Curtain*]

ACT TWO

SCENE ONE

FRED *tight and dapper. Bills in one hand. White trousers.*

FRED:
Well, folks, we been up and down these Chinatown hills sucking up
the sights faster'n the eye can see.

You've seen the medicinal chicken cure impotence in males.
The quick Kung Fu spit hit a brick and break it in two.
The Chickencoop Chinaman make whooppee in a birdcage.
The highbinder squint at tits.
The sidewinder caress a shoe.
And lots of silky butt paddlefooted fools dance the willies for a dime.
You've seen the fan tan and got a nickel shine
From a Chinaman albino the color of Spam.

And now your eyes are inwards on your innards.
You're hungry, folks.
Hungry! And afraid to eat anything here.
I know the feeling . . . Bad feeling . . .
                              [*Curtain*]

SCENE TWO

Eng family apartment. Predawn. CHINA MAMA *is asleep on the
couch.*
     FRED *comes in cussing under his breath. Bushed. He turns on*

the TV, sits at the kitchen table, takes off his jacket. Lights a couple of punks and burns them in the shrine. From the shrine he takes down an old tin box. He sits at the kitchen table, watches TV, and starts to roll a joint.

CHINA MAMA *gets up and goes to the stove. She gets* FRED *a bowl of rice, a side dish, and a cup of tea from a thermos jug. She moves the tin box of pot aside.*

CHINA MAMA: Sick luh, ah-jie! (*"Eat, son."*)

FRED: Huh?

CHINA MAMA: Nay doe kee um doe kee, uh?

FRED: You want me to be Chinese too, huh? Everybody does . . . You know how the tourists tell I'm Chinese? No first person pronouns. No "I," "Me" or "We." I talk like that lovable sissy, Charlie Chan, no first person personal pronouns, and instant Chinese culture . . . ha, ha, ha . . . (*Motions* CHINA MAMA *to sit*) English lesson, China Mama. How do you say "English" in Chinese.

CHINA MAMA: Mutt yeh? (*Hands* FRED *chopsticks*)

FRED (*puts chopsticks down*): "Ying mun" lesson, uhh "Yup jick" citizenship you uhh gotta talk some "Ying mun," huh? Huh?

CHINA MAMA: Huh?

FRED: "I" (FRED *points to himself. Nods to* CHINA MAMA, *urging her to repeat with him*) "I"! . . .

CHINA MAMA: "I" (*Points to her eye*)

SIS (*appears from the hallway; she wears a bathrobe and is half awake*): Hi . . . I thought it was you . . .

FRED (*overlapping*): Jeeziz Christ, ma's been teachin her English!

SIS: All of us have been teaching China Mama English. There was nothing else to do with you out . . .

FRED (*holds up his fingers as if making a number one*): "I . . . !"

CHINA MAMA (*repeats* FRED's *gesture*): "I!"

SIS: What are you doing at this hour?

FRED: Teachin China Mama first person *personal* pronouns . . . You'll make her a citizen. But I'll give ya depth, soul . . .

SIS (*having never stopped*): . . . anyone in the bathroom?

FRED: No.

SIS (*having never stopped; under*): I'll find out for myself . . . (*Goes into the bathroom*)

FRED (*points his index finger straight up, making the number one*): "I" (*Points the number one finger at himself*) "I"

CHINA MAMA (*makes the number one and points to* FRED): "I!"

FRED (*points up, makes the number one, emphatically*): I! (*Points to* CHINA MAMA) . . . is *you!* You going "I" is *you!* Not me . . . (*Points to himself*) I say "I" is me!

CHINA MAMA: "Me"

FRED (*points up, making the number one*): "I"

CHINA MAMA (*jabs her finger up*): I!

FRED (*points to himself; louder*): "Me . . ."

CHINA MAMA: "Me . . . !" (*Points to herself*)

FRED (*spreads his arms; louder*): We!

CHINA MAMA (*embraces* FRED): "We!" . . .

FRED: All the tourists act the same when they hear me spring my first person pronouns, China Mama . . . (*Gets* CHINA MAMA *off him*) "I. Me. We." You are now a citizen, congratulations . . . I'm not Chinese. This ain't China. Your language is foreign and ugly to me, so how come you're my mother? (*Reads total noncomprehension in* CHINA MAMA's *face*) I mean, I don't think I'm quite your idea of a son, either . . . You hear all my first person pronouns, China Mama. They're glistening in my natural talk like stars. Me and ma and Sis get together and we're talkin a universe, and sing . . . Talkin to you, China Mama. China Mama, I wanta ask you a question . . . What has happened to Annette Funicello? See? You don't laugh . . .

(CHINA MAMA *goes to the sink, gets a plastic tub from under the sink, fills it with hot water and brings it over to* FRED *and sticks his feet in as he continues . . .*)

FRED (*having never stopped*): You don't know what I'm doing . . . well, ma don't know what I'm doing but she knows when I mean to be funny. I was gonna be somebody "special," not "spesul" like pa says, but "special," see? I don't know the word for that either . . . You're just another tourist wanting me to be

Chinese, China Mama. Just because we're born here don't mean we're nobody and gotta go away to another language to talk. I think Chinatown Buck Buck Bagaw is beautiful.

(CHINA MAMA *rolls joints out of* FRED's *tin box. She lights up and smokes joints like cigarettes*.)

FRED: . . . Maybe it's only for reaching some loonies and my family but we're real. Chinatown's as real as China. Not as big. But really, I'm impressed. A Chinese mother . . . (*Sees* CHINA MAMA *smoking. Takes the joint from her. Gets up and lights more punk*) Yin see, China Mama . . . (*He takes a long toke*.)

SIS (*comes out of the bathroom*): Yin see's "opium" Fred . . .

FRED: I know I don't know how to talk Chinese, but this is an emergency, Sis.

(CHINA MAMA *takes the joint from* FRED *and, likewise, takes a long toke*.)

SIS: Don't I know "when you mean to be funny" as well as ma? (*Joins* FRED *and* CHINA MAMA *at the table*)

FRED: Better, Sis . . . Oh, you better take a hit. I think she thinks it's the custom in America . . .

SIS (*takes the joint and passes it to* FRED): Oh, I don't want this stuff so early in the morning . . . Where have you been all this time, cuddling with your lady tourists?

(CHINA MAMA *returns to her place and lights up a joint*.)

FRED: That and playing hide'n'seek with Johnny. (*Sees* CHINA MAMA *smoking*) No! China Mama dat's not yin jie? Not . . . what the hell? Bad! China Mama!

SIS *and* FRED (*ad lib*): Bad! No good! Mo! Um ho! Bad!

SIS: He's come home every night . . .

FRED: I wanta talk to him alone. But he won't talk to me. I think you scared him.

SIS: The reason he won't talk to you is because *I* scared him . . .?

FRED: That business about forgetting Chinatown to become "just people."

SIS: Why would that scare anybody . . .

FRED (*having never stopped*): . . . cuz out there we'll become nobody.

SIS: Fred . . . you'll be able to write at least.

FRED: Everybody'll be too busy to bother with me. Becoming a nobody's a hell of a lot to look forward to, Sis . . . Here we're somebody . . .

SIS: Rats, goodie goods, cowards, crybabies, failures, nice Charlie
Chans . . .

FRED: "We respect Charlie Chan. He was superior to whites cuz he
kept his hands at his sides and never said 'I,' 'Me,' or 'We' . . ."

SIS: We're different, Fred, remember?

FRED: "Confucius was a Chinese. You should be proud to be Chinese, dear . . ."

SIS: We're the pioneers. You and me, Jr. Texas Ranger . . .

FRED: I don't wanta be a pioneer. Just a writer. Just see my name in
a book by me. About things I like writing about, and fuck the pioneers. What've the old pioneers done for us, for me? I'm not even
fighting nobody. I just have a few words and they come at me.
"Be Chinese, Charlie Chan or a nobody" to the whites and a mad
dog to the Chinamans . . . for what? To die and be discovered by
some punk in the next generation and published in mimeograph
by some college ethnic studies department, forget it. I have to
take care of myself now. I have to protect my . . .

SIS: From what . . .

FRED: From you. From the family, everyone . . . Pa has a point,
don't do nothin and don't tell anybody what you're doing . . .

SIS: And what happens to the family, Fred?

FRED: For me, I've been thinking.

(CHINA MAMA *pours a shot or glug of booze into* FRED's *footbath.*
FRED *watches.*)

ROSS (*appears from the hallway; he's in a bathrobe and waking up*):
What's everybody doing up at this hour?

FRED: Take Johnny back with ya and after pa's gone, it'll be a
little. . .

SIS: No, Fred. If I take Johnny in at all, it's with the understanding
that you're getting the family out of Chinatown like you say
you've always wanted and take over your share of the business . . .
No more of your little deals . . .

ROSS (*overlapping* SIS): Mama Fu Fu's is expanding into frozen food
. . .

SIS (*having never stopped*): I'm not going to be used as Johnny's babysitter. If I'm no more to you than that . . . I don't want any more money . . .

FRED: Who're you telling me . . . She like this with you, Ross? . . . That's your dream, not mine, Sis . . .

SIS (*overlapping*): I've paid for the right to tell you a thing or two. I've worked as hard as you. Now don't tell me to sweep the floor or sing a song . . .

FRED: Sis, I helped you out of here . . .

SIS: And I'm trying to help you. Johnny's not going to leave without you, you know that.

FRED: You know what you're asking me to do, Sis? Chinatown is my private bok gwai redhead of the week club . . .

ROSS: Now we're very fond of your family, Fred . . .

SIS (*cutting* ROSS *off*): You don't owe pa anything. You're the head of the family. You owe Johnny. You owe me . . .

FRED: You owe me! I put you through talking my guts out funny all over the fucking streets. You owe me . . .

SIS: All I owe you is money; I'll be glad to pay you back every cent, with interest. Just say the word and I'll write you a check.

CHINA MAMA (*stoned; breaks into song*):
> Sing Song, Sing Song, So Hop Toy . . .
> Alle same like China Boy.
> But he sellee girl with joy.
> Pity poor Ming Toy . . .

MA (*from the bedroom, overlapping*): What's goin on out there?

FRED: Ma do this? I gotta get some sleep before my morning tour. Everything'll be okay, Sis, believe me . . . I'll be down at the office . . .

SIS: Forget tours. That part of your life's over. Just say so, Fred. What do you think I've been working for?

ROSS: Oh, we're going to be big, whether you join us or not. Right, honey? A chain of Mama Fu Fu's. Franchises. Mail order . . . A syndicated column . . . Frozen food . . .

SIS: Take the day off. Go lie down. Ross is taking the whole family out to lunch.

FRED (*overlapping*): I can't make it. I gotta special noon tour.

SIS: Fred, if you're not going to take me seriously . . .

FRED: I like doing tours, Sis.

SIS: You're kidding. Why? You're no Chinatown queer.

(FRED *puts on shoes.*)

FRED: Doing tours is the only way I can get outta here without . . .

SIS: You can get outta here. This is crazy . . . It's not like you to be so wishy washy . . .

FRED: You're the one who made it big, Sis. I'm not starving, and for me, I talk out loud to myself walking up and down the streets of Chinatown and I'm gone. Outta town. No interruptions. On the Interstate. No arguments. I'm poppin the high rhythm six step of a tuned compact car, and I know where everything is . . .

MA (*enters from hallway; she wears a bathrobe and goes to the bathroom*): I'll make coffee in a minute . . . (*Hums a cowboy tune while* FRED *speaks*)

FRED (*having never stopped*): What part of the car's my little finger . . . I keep talking, and I feel the whine of the tires echo up my asshole, into my spine, my ribs, into my throat and I have the shoulders of a tiger, the reflexes of an IBM and I am, as long as I'm talking, out of here, running up the road on my hands and feet!

SIS: The Chinatown Cowboy rides again!

FRED: Sis!

MA (*overlapping, inside the bathroom*): Oh? I would've said he was a Buick Riviera.

FRED: Don't ya know what I'm talking about? All I think about is what I'm gonna feel like out there. But I'm afraid I'll give up my dream out there . . .

SIS: You'll feel like yourself out there.

MA: I thought he said he felt like a "compact car."

FRED: What's wrong, ma?

MA: Nothing.

SIS (*overlapping*): Your writing used to win awards . . .

FRED: Still nobody publishes it.

SIS: Here, you don't even write anymore. You're just a tourist guide!

FRED: Oh, ho ho! Sissy's come home! That's my dream, Sis. But I'm afraid I'll get out there. Pick up my pen. And it dies. I'll have nothing.

SIS: You'll have the family . . . Fred . . .

FRED: We'll work something out tonight. I promise, Sis. (*To* ROSS) Sign my name to the tab after lunch. On me, okay? (*To* SIS) Now come on, gimme a hug, my fine Mama Fu Fu. (FRED *and* SIS *embrace*.) For what it's worth, I'm proud of ya, Sissy.

> (FRED *goes out the door* . . .)

FRED *and* SIS (SIS *joins late*): God's gift to sluts strikes again . . . !

SIS (*after* FRED *has left*): Oh, god, Ross. I wish we'd never come . . .

[Curtain]

SCENE THREE

Chopsticks. Day. FRED *appears at* JOHNNY's *side and does not like what he sees and hears.* JOHNNY's *accent is more exaggerated than* FRED's.

JOHNNY: So, okay, allaw you folkses, 'faw goings inner resernt faw eat up lotsa delife ful seepesulty da house Chinese highlights obba tour . . .

FRED (*trying to cop the action*): Dis's is Fred Eng, "Freddie . . ."

JOHNNY: . . . and John Eng, "Johnny" onna . . .

FRED *and* JOHNNY: . . . behalf obba Eng Chinatowng Tour'n'Travooo . . .

> (FRED *and* JOHNNY *exchange glances*.)

FRED: Saying.

FRED *and* JOHNNY: . . . Tang you . . .

FRED: . . . daw jeh!

JOHNNY (*grins at* FRED): . . . and goong hay fot choy take da look roung whiff me!

> (FRED *and* JOHNNY *take chopsticks out of their inside jacket pockets. They trade lines.*)

FRED: Please take these chopsticks, . . .

JOHNNY: . . . anna eat you dinner wid it.

FRED: You wanna some a ex'ras send away for friends or foes jussa asking me . . .

JOHNNY: . . . or me.

FRED: Now . . .

(*The more* JOHNNY *enjoys the spiel, the more* FRED *comes down . . .*)

JOHNNY: . . . how eat widdie tings you're mebe asking mos' like, huh? Me heap sahbay! Okay! Looka dis! See . . . You're hol'ing one dis stick like dis, making it stiff, donk can move roung anywhere, okay? Whaddat goot for, you're mebe asking now . . .

FRED (*finally takes over in rhythm*): Den dis udder ones is like a pensoo. Hol' it like you maybe catchum write love letter, okay, lady? Me longtime Calley Foorn! An' lookie how you're move stick all likee dis? Okay?

(FRED *and* JOHNNY *hold up chopsticks and work them a few times.*)

FRED *and* JOHNNY: Okay? Okay? Allaw okays? Ever'bolly okays? Okay! Okay? (*Bowing out*) Goodbye. Okay? Okay! Goodbye. Okay. Goodbye. Goodbye . . .

FRED (*going off; under his breath*): Goddam motherfucking, cocksucking spongy green rat puke sonofabitchin . . .

JOHNNY (*overlapping*): Yeah! Ha. Ha. Ha. That was a good tour! Yeah . . . (*Goes off ahead of* FRED *into the apartment.* JOHNNY *changes from his sports jacket into kid outfit.*)

FRED: Johnny!

JOHNNY: I'll seeya at home . . .

(JOHNNY *leaves.*)

[*Curtain*]

Eng family apartment. Noon. JOHNNY *and* FRED *enter from outside.*

FRED: Didya hear me with Ross? I can't even get pissed-off at a white man without my voice drifting off into some movie, like a reflex . . .

JOHNNY: Come on, man. You wanta talk to me or not? Too moochie shiyet!

FRED: Pa says it's okay for you to go to college.

JOHNNY: He didn't say nothing to you. I could hear it . . .

FRED (*having never stopped, goes on*): Ma and me'll be out right after . . .

> (FRED *goes to bedroom.*)

JOHNNY (*cuts* FRED *off*): Naw, you wanna go. I'll do the tour'n'travel for ya. Pa'll help me with what . . . you know . . . Lemme helpya out, Fred. I'll take care of China Mama . . .

FRED (*from bedroom*): Don't you worry bout China Mama. Worry bout yourself.

JOHNNY (*overlapping* FRED'*s last line*): I'll put on that new suit you got me and go out withya tomorrow . . .

FRED (*comes out with a suitcase and a bunch of clothes*): Take the day off. Your probation's up. Start packing. (*He starts packing Johnny's suitcase.*)

JOHNNY: Listen, Fred, you been working hard for me ever since I was five. I wanta do something for *you*, man . . . I'll helpya out of Chinatown . . .

FRED: You'll help me? I don't wanta hear it! Goddamn! . . . You! Trying to con *me*!

JOHNNY: You taught me how to talk like you, you gave me a car. I know what you did for me . . .

FRED: "You gave me a car." Willya quit the con, just quit it. Who do you think I am? You ain't gonna . . . I hate tourist guides! I taught you to hate tourist guides. We're not tourist guides any more!

JOHNNY: Fred . . . Fred . . .

FRED: I'm goin crazy round here, but you! You're so stupid, you

think I'm stupid. You're carrying toys . . . Chinese New Year's.
A million cops out there.

JOHNNY: Hey, man, everybody's got guns . . .

FRED: "Hey, man, everybody's got guns"! Come into your own
home. Try to con me. I oughta see you busted! Where's that
phone . . . (*Goes for the phone*)

JOHNNY: Fred, don't . . . (*Gets a hand on the phone*) It would kill
pa . . .

FRED: My pa. Him finally gone might make us feel at home
again . . .

JOHNNY: You motherfucker. You quit talking like that.

FRED: Go to college, Johnny. Go back east to college. If you come
back to Chinatown afterwards as a Chinatown tourist guide, okay.
I want ya to see another movie for a while, that's all. See something else. Get a white girl while you're young. You'll never regret it. You know, learn to feel at home somewhere
else . . . Later me and ma will come out.

JOHNNY: I don't know nothing bout being "at home" man. All I know
at home is you.

FRED: Huh?

JOHNNY: I got everything you ever said about Chinatown in my
head. But out here *is* Chinatown and it's not what you talked. But
I think it is, you know? I feel like some freak of evolution here,
man. I don't know what it feels like to be "at home" the way you
talk about to the bok gwai, or ma or Sissy . . .

FRED: Back east, Johnny, Boston. Go get some new pictures. It's
old, historic. Just colleges all over the place. . . .

JOHNNY: The only time I ever relaxed in my life I was driving a car
full of robbers, man. I didn't know what that Chinese they was
talking. But I knew I was doing what they told me, when I drove
away from that store. Felt so goood.

FRED: What is this, some oral report? What've I been raisin here?
Shit! You'd think when I was being serious, you'd at least . . .

JOHNNY: You shuddup! I'm being serious! Lemme tell you something for a change. Things happened to me too! In my life! I can
talk too, god fuckit, I got stories! (*Stalks around the room breathing heavy*) Damn! (*Stalks the quiet*) DAMN, FRED! . . . I was in

my car full of masked robbers talking Chinese I couldn't understand. My Chevvy was flying down Grant Avenue, man. We
musta beendoing sixty. And I smoked cigars wit doze dudes. I
bashed a language I can't speak. I made friends, man, and didn't
give a fuck. I stole wit'em. And drove their getaways for them,
and never stopped talking back to them in a language I don't give
a damn about.

FRED: What?

JOHNNY (*having never stopped, goes on*): . . . I didn't care if I
talked Chinese fine enough to make'em treat me like shit, man.
Making sense to them never crossed my mind. If they were gonna
shoot me, I didn't give a nickel shine. I was gonna have me a good
time with the rest of my life. And talking any kind of Chinese at
all is a good time, Fred.

FRED: Whadda you know about Chinese?

JOHNNY: Nothing! I'm stupid! . . . But I believe in the Chinese family.

FRED: What Chinese family? Do you mean China Mama? Or you
mean my police chief special explaining our lack of juvenile delinquency in the fifties? That Chinese family isn't real, Johnny . . .

JOHNNY: That's what I like about you, Fred. You don't give a shit.
The way you style lies to them tourists. Don't I know you can do a
story like that in a flash? But I lived that story for real. What's the
last time you did that?

FRED: What?

JOHNNY (*having never stopped*): I'm no tourist! I'm your brother!

FRED: . . . And your brother is shit. I am shit. This family is shit.
Chinatown's shit. You can't love each other around here without
hating yourself. But you got it. You and Sis got it. Please lemme
helpya Johnny. Believe me just this once . . .

JOHNNY: Fred, if I was a writer, man. I'd write a story and make you
king . . .

FRED: "King?"

JOHNNY (*having never stopped*): . . . and I'd be the writer of the
realm, and ma and pa wouldn't mind you being King . . .

FRED: King. I tellya I'm no good and you wanta make me King.

JOHNNY: You go be a writer. I wanta do tours for pa. That's all.

FRED (*incredulous*): What? "For pa"? You wanta use the tours as a front to make suey shops pay . . .

JOHNNY: Listen, Fred. Come on. Honest, now. We both know I know things we don't wanta talk about, right? You can bust me, okay . . . Everybody callin me stupid and lazy and a bum and pa don't take me out to lunch in town, like he does you, or even stay on the same side of the street . . .

FRED: Being a tourist guide won't fix that . . .

JOHNNY: But we're supposed to be together, fool!

FRED: Leave me out of it! You wanta stay in Chinatown? Stay and rot. To hell with all of ya . . .

JOHNNY: Just til pa dies . . . then I'll do whatever, man . . .

FRED: No, you just remember who raised ya. Who covered for ya . . .

JOHNNY: Fred, I wanta be a part of this family when pa kicks, not a bum!

FRED (*starts to say something but stops; he flops into a chair*): You gotta get to that lunch. Pa'n'everybody's waiting . . .

JOHNNY (*at the door, ready to go*): You comin, Fred?

FRED (*motions Johnny out*): No, I . . . uhhh . . .

(JOHNNY *goes out the door. A long string of firecrackers goes off outside. Lion drums and cymbals. Oooh, chatter and laughter from the crowd outside.* FRED *broods oblivious to the noise outside. He leaves.*)

[*Curtain*]

SCENE FIVE

Eng family apartment. Night of the parade. The back wall has been cleared of the stand-up wardrobe and pile of newspapers. Two matching chairs with very high straight backs are set in the center of the wall. They are separated by a low table. A small stack of mandarin oranges—each with at least a leaf and a bit of stem showing—is arranged in a pyramid on the table. PA *sits in one chair. He's dressed in a bathrobe, slippers, and underwear. He's wearing his glasses and reading his speech.*

Above on the wall is a piece of framed calligraphy saying "The Mayor of Chinatown" in large Chinese characters. It is composed horizontally.

MA has done her hair in a style too young for her. She's dressed in a tight cheongsam, and is playing the part of a Chinese woman as authentically as she can, which means she's Susie Wong and Flower Drum Song.

SIS and ROSS are listening to PA rehearse his speech.

ROSS is posing the family for picture-taking. SIS is icing the champagne in the sink. CHINA MAMA is seated to PA's left.

VOICE: Sin dah Ninetee' fi'ty fi'e Sahm Fa'nsicko der Chinatown mos' famoused worl' famous Chinese New Year *anywhere*, celebrate inna whole worl', lady anner gennuhmans! GOONG HAY FOT CHOY da Year's obber Draggons!

SIS: Oh, the parade's started already, pa! Let's go, Fred can meet us at the stand . . .

PA: Da's okay. Wait for Fred.

SIS: Well, we can't wait much longer and still see the parade. Ross has never seen a real dragon.

ROSS (*placing SIS and MA in the picture*): Mattie, right here, honey. And ma, over here. That cheongsam is perfect . . .

PA: Should be a jacket . . . ?

ROSS: No . . . No . . . Fine.

SIS: Save your strength for your speech, pa.

VOICE: Kickoff tonigh wit da Border Rectors Chinee Cham'er Commerce in a Caddie-lax, folks! Hubba! Hubba!

ROSS (*overlapping, snapping shots*): Now one more.

PA (*waves MA and SIS out of the picture brusquely; to SIS*): You wanna see porly? Look outta window, you see it. (*Gives an extra prod to a reluctant MA then turns to ROSS*) Ma! Maybe you teck like dis . .
Chinese family . . . (*Indicates him and CHINA MAMA sitting in straight-backed chairs*)

ROSS: Okay, China Mama . . . mo yook . . .

CHINA MAMA: Huh?

PA: He saying you mo yook!

SIS: Aren't you supposed to be riding in the parade now, pa?

(ROSS *snaps picture*.)

PA: Ride da pourlay too much drafty. No goo. (*To* ROSS) Now teck nudder . . . Put on jacket fois! (*Rises to get jacket*) No ride no porly now. Ha. Ha. Ha. Wait faw Fred we allaw go togedders . . .

ROSS: You look fine, Ngawk Fu . . .

PA: Naw! Naw! . . . No jecket look too dorty. Uckly . . .

VOICE (*ad lib; covering* PA *putting on jacket, sitting*): Kip da onner curbs ladies anner gennuhmans, here coming dah ache Immortals . . .

PA (*sitting for his picture with* CHINA MAMA): Sure! Sure! Look becker now . . .

(MA *goes to* PA *and sits on his lap*.)

MA: How about something like this, Ross? "The Best of the East and the Best of the West." (*Kisses* PA *on the forehead*)

PA (*moves* MA *off his lap, wipes his head*): Ma! (*To* ROSS) Okay. How looking?

VOICE: Ache Immortal like Chinee Seven Dwarf no Snow Whites! Ha ha ha! Goong Hay . . . !

(ROSS *snaps picture*.)

PA: Okay nudder one now . . . (*Poses*) Okay, we listen spitch, one maw time, okay? Wait faw Fred?

ROSS: Oh, sure . . .

SIS (*overlapping*): Quiet, everybody . . . Shh. Shhh.

VOICE: Dah Sak-raymen doe Chinee Schoo' Drear tim Marchie Ban, folks!

PA (*reading from his prepared speech*): "Befaw rad dah terrorgram fum der Presden Rubber Nighted Steaks Sum Erika, lemme be like Cholly Chan Deteckive one moo-er" . . . Murmer? (*To* ROSS) "Moomum." How dat?

(JOHNNY *comes in the front door*.)

MA: It's on the stove son.

ROSS: "Moment."

JOHNNY: Whyn'tya at the parade?

SIS: We can't go without Fred. Where is he anyway?

JOHNNY: It's Chinese New Years.

(CHINA MAMA *helps* PA *off with his jacket and carefully hangs it up*.)

ROSS: "Moe ment."

PA: Yeah. "An . . . Uhh . . . inn reduced ding . . ." (MA *races for* CHINA MAMA's *empty seat next to* PA.)

MA: All human beings are people, don't you think so, Ross? You're as Chinese as me and I'm as American as you and Pa's . . . as . . .

PA: Ma! What nex' I asking you? Haaa! (*Motions* MA *off chair. Returns to speech*)

   (MA *goes to the bathroom and kicks things a little.* CHINA MAMA *returns to her seat*.)

PA: "An' inn reduced ding tar you tonigh Year da Dragger, dah one who're teck obber solve dah case. My's Nummer One Son, allaw time, saying 'Gee, Pop!' Fred Eng!"

   (SIS *and* ROSS *cheer and applaud, chuckle*.)

SIS *and* ROSS (*ad lib*): Oh, yes . . . very funny . . .

PA: I rid dat awright? . . . "Now my onna bore presents to you this ton . . ." Tom? Tahhh.

ROSS: "Time." Tie-yumm.

PA: "Tahhh . . . Yummm" . . .

VOICE: Here come dah Yerng Wah color gar' anna Marchin Ban' Folks.

ROSS: "It is now my honor to present at this time . . ."

PA: Yeah, da's right. (*Looks at speech in his hands*) Jus' like it say, right here ha ha ha . . . Johnny . . . He'pping me get ready now. Fred come we go . . .

JOHNNY: Sure, pa.

ROSS: You don't know how thrilling for me, A Ngawk Fu . . . This has really been one of the most exciting three days in my life. I didn't really believe it when Mattie said she was the only Chinese who could ever like me . . . Because, you know, I've always admired the superiority of Chinese culture.

SIS: Ma, come on out here and make Ross feel at home.

MA (*coming out of the bathroom*): I didn't mean to make you think I was being hostile.

SIS: Aww, ma, we know you're not hostile . . .

MA: I better helpya, Johnny, before you clumsy oaf give pa a black eye. Okay pa?

PA: Hostew? Who hostew my spitch?

SIS: Pa, it's a wonderful speech.

PA: Good spitch, huh?

ROSS: Everyone's going to love your speech, Ngawk Fu. You don't have to worry about hostility in Chinatown . . . on Chinese New Year's. Now me, I'm used to hostility.

MA: I'm so sorry to hear that . . .

ROSS (*overlapping*): Women hate me. Homosexuals hate me . . .

SIS (*under*): Oh, Ross!

ROSS (*having never stopped*): Hawks hate me. Doves. Republicans, Communists, Democrats, Southern Whites. Freedom riders. Blacks. Chicanos, Indians, hardhats. Ecologists. The police . . . ! I'm Mr. White Male Supremacist. Middle Middle class American liberal Four Years of College Pig. So I'm used to hostility. Ha. Ha. Even dogs I've never met hate me. I'm walking down the street and see a Hare Krishna chanter . . .

PA: Har Krish?

SIS: Oh, no . . .

ROSS (*having never stopped, goes on*): Yeah, I see a Hare Krishna chanter grinning seductively at me. I step aside, to walk around him instead of knocking him down and walking over him like he expects me to do.

SIS: Like you want to do.

ROSS: Like I want to do . . . And I step into a pile of dogshit the size of an angel food cake. (*To* MA) Excuse me. So I know hostility. It's an old friend. And you're not hostile. You're the most wonderful people I've ever known.

MA (*overlapping*): You hearie that, young man?

SIS (*overlapping* MA): "Hearie"?

MA: So polite!

JOHNNY: Yeah, ma.

PA: When dat guy grows up, I asking you. (*Strips bathrobe*) . . . Donor runt.

MA: Aw, Wing he's a good boy.

   (JOHNNY *lifts* PA's *arms and sprays his armpits with deodorant.*)

PA: I been happy wit' you, ma.

VOICE: Da Saint Mary Gir drills teams, folks! Looka dose costume! Dese Sain' Mary Chinee school gir's are be da olden time China-town worl' fame traditions, folks!

MA: Aw, whaddaya talking?

(FRED *comes in the front door. His cussing is drowned out by the voice.*)

VOICE: A big han'! Goong hay! Goong hay fot choy!

PA: Where'se you be? Youfawget? (*To* JOHNNY) Red shirt, lucky . . .

(JOHNNY *gets* PA's *red shirt and helps him on with it.*)

PA (*to* FRED): Well, get my shoe, can't you? Be useful . . . ! Huh, son?

(JOHNNY *gets* PA's *shoes.*)

MA (*knuckle-raps* FRED *on the head*): How come so late?

FRED: Huh? . . . I was worried you'd all be gone. Here's some cham-pagne. Misser da Mayors o' Chinatowng! You okay, ma?

PA: Jussie like a lew kit! When're you're grown up? Sure I wait for you. You come home . . . (*To* JOHNNY) Pants . . . Den we go. Den I mecking my spitch! Allaw happy!

(JOHNNY *gets* PA's *trousers and tries to slip them on while* MA *tries to get socks on* PA's *feet.*)

ROSS: Then we all clap! Yeah. Applause!

(*All clap.*)

SIS (*overlapping clapping*): Oh, Pa, it'll sound so good out there, echoing over the street . . .

PA: Hey, son! You got dah case solve yet?

(PA, SIS, ROSS, *and* MA *laugh.*)

FRED (*brushing it off*): Huh? Yeah, sure, pa. Your probation's up, Johnny. Time to fly the coop. I'm firing you now . . .

JOHNNY: What're you talkin?

PA (*overlapping*): No, "Pa" . . . "Pop!" son.

JOHNNY (*answering* FRED, *covering* PA): Dis is my home! You're the one told me . . .

FRED: Come on, Johnny.

PA: Call me "Pop"!

JOHNNY (*having never stopped, goes on*): . . . living in Chinatown's an art, man. Well, dig it, punk. I'm an artist.

FRED: A deal's a deal, kid. I kept my end.

JOHNNY: I'm telling ya forget it. Hey, pa, you gonna let Fred fire me? There ain't no Boston.

PA: "Pop."

FRED: Pa, I wanta talk . . .

PA (*overlapping*): "Pop" son. Call me "Pop."

FRED (*overlapping*): I wanta talk to you , pa . . .

PA: Call me "Pop"!

FRED: "Pop"? What is this "Pop"?

> (*All but* FRED *titter and chuckle.*)

PA: Sure! You my Nummer One Son? Yes or no? Yes!

FRED: You been drinking?

PA: Den you're calling me "Pop." "Gosh, Pop!" "Gee, Pop!"

FRED: Pa been drinking?

PA: Pop! Drink later. After my spitch!

FRED: Then what's this case he . . .

SIS: Charlie Chan! Detective? Number One Son? Case?

ROSS: Charlie Chan.

FRED: Pa's told his first joke without a word of Chinese in it! His first all-American joke! . . . Wonderful pa!

MA: What's so wonderful about that. Pa's Chinese yes or no? Huh, "Pop"?

FRED: Ma?

SIS: We've been laughing at it all day.

ROSS: He says he'd like you to sit up on the reviewing stand next to him and . . . (*Indicates* CHINA MAMA)

FRED: Me? Well, what about ma?

SIS: He wants you there so he can use the joke in his speech.

JOHNNY: Tell Chinatown you're his Number One Son.

FRED: Tell Chinatown I'm your Number One Son?

PA: Den drunk later, after spitch. Celebrate. Ha. Ha . . . (*To* JOHNNY) Breath. (*To* MA) Feet.

> (JOHNNY *and* MA *follow* PA's *instructions.*)

SIS: You know what that Charlie Chan joke means, Freddie?

FRED: It means we fucked up, huh, ma? It's okay my little spongy green . . .

MA (*knuckle-rap*): Oh, you watch you mouth!

ROSS (*overlapping*): It means you've made it, Fred.

FRED (*overlapping*): What's wrong, ma? "Whassie la mallaw"?

MA: Don't ya feel like singing and dancing tonight, son?

SIS: Oh, Freddie, we're going to have champagne and go to the parade and hear pa's speech . . .

MA: Don't ya wanta dance with ma tonight?

FRED: Been drinking, ma? "Whalla mallaw"?

MA: . . . Or don't you dare?

PA (*overlapping*): Drunk later, all togedders, ma . . . Johnny not ol' nuff, but tonight okay, okay? Okay. China Mama, Sissy, dah husban' . . .

MA (*wagging her finger at* FRED): Whallamalla! So hop toy . . .

PA (*overlapping, under*): "So hop toy"?

(PA *exchanges looks with* CHINA MAMA.)

CHINA MAMA: "So hop toy"?

MA: Yeah. "So hop toy"! So what?

FRED: What's "So hop toy"?

JOHNNY: "So hop toy" hie um hie yung wah, ah bah!

CHINA MAMA: Talkie Chinee!

PA: "So hop toy"? Chinee? No.

CHINA MAMA: "So hop toy"?

MA: Hey, granpa!

FRED: "Ah-goong goong," ma . . .

MA: Ah goong goong ah! You wanna boy or girl?

CHINA MAMA: Ah! "So hop toy!" (*Pats* PA *and turns to* MA *and sings*)
                    Sing song, sing song.

ALL (*joining in*):
                    So Hop Toy!
    (*All crack up laughing.*)

MA (*sings on; she takes out a fan and does a slinky, mincing, head bobbing, pointy-this pointy-that dance as she sings*):
            Sing song, sing song, So Hop Toy.
            Allee same like China Boy.
            But he sellee girl with joy.
            Pity poor Ming Toy . . .
    (*As* MA *sings,* FRED *hustles her firmly but gently to the bathroom. He sings the song with her.*)

FRED (*seats her on the toilet, while he wets a rag; he wipes her face, fixes her hair*): Hey, where's my girl? Come on my American of Chinese descent, huh?

SIS (*hands bottle of champagne to* JOHNNY): Here Johnny, open this up for pa. He has to save his strength for his speech. Come on, everybody.

(*All except* FRED *and* MA *gather round* JOHNNY *while* JOHNNY *uncorks the champagne.*)

PA: Where ma?

SIS: Come on, you two! We're going to toast the Year of the Dragon.

PA: Bat'room. Allaw time bat'room.

FRED: Hold your horses. (*Turns to* MA *and searches her face for comprehension*) "Hole your horses," ma? "Criminy sakes"? "Psycho spasmatic"? Hello, Hyacinth, how's tricks?

MA: Nobody's called me Hyacinth in years.

FRED: "Calling all cars."

MA (*a little remote*): Donk hate your pa for the bigamist he're be, son. I've made up my mind.

FRED (*smiling, relieved*): Aw, naw, ma . . .

MA (*having never stopped*): I've lived here with pa since I was only fifteen years old . . .

FRED (*joshing*): You've been living here with me, too, since you were fifteen ma. Didn't I give you hemorrhoids?

MA: I just looked at him awhile ago and he look so beautiful. He was like flowers you see shimmer up their smell on a hot day. I never seen you that way. And all I could do was act silly when I was you ma. You pa's right . . .

FRED: Ma, you're a realist and he's a dreamer . . .

MA: I've never seen anything so beautiful like pa just now. I bet he had lots of girlfriends behind my back, but I'm too stupid to see that shimmer til just now . . .

ROSS: Hey, Jeff Foo! Come out here for some Goong Hay Fot Choy!

MA: I wish I was you real ma. But China Mama . . .

FRED: It's okay. Don't say anything else . . .

MA: I'm no liar. I didn't mean to lie to anybody. Specially you . . .

FRED: Ma . . .

MA: I think it's important for you to hear it from me. I'm not your real ma.

FRED (*blanks a moment*): . . . Ma. I know that. Everybody knew that. And everybody told me. But . . . you. You should not have told me. No, ma. I'd joke about it, I'd tell everybody else, but I would never have told you . . . as a straight . . . man, I would never *tell* you I'm . . . because I am . . . But you just tole me I'm *not* your son, didn't you? And ha! Look, ma, I haven't disappeared, or got short of breath or . . . I'm still me. Still forty years old.

MA: Huh?

FRED: It was like surviving a mild electric shock. See? Still me.

MA: Huh?

FRED: Still you. Ha. Come on, champagne out here . . . (*Helps* MA *out of the bathroom*)

ALL (*except* FRED *and* MA, *to* FRED *and* MA): Hey! Goong Hay Fot Choy!

FRED: Sure! Goong hay fot choy.

PA: Okay! One toas' den we go. My speech tonight, huh, ma?

   (*All but* MA *laugh low and congenially.*)

PA: Ma?

   (PA *lifts his glass. All lift their glasses.*)

PA: Da dragger have a head like a pa mow, a camels, hairs like a lahng manes, body liking snakes, fin an' tails like fish, foot like a tigers, clar like a eagles anna run dong Chinatowng on tennie shoe!

   (*All but* MA *chuckle.*)

PA: Nudder joke, son! Goong hay fot choy!

ALL: Goong hay fot choy! (*All drink.*)

   (ROSS *hands* FRED *a red envelope.* SIS *stands by.*)

ROSS: Goong hay fot choy . . . I hope this is satisfactory . . .

FRED: Keep your money.

ROSS: If it's not enough . . .

FRED: Keep your money . . .

SIS: Does that mean you're coming?

FRED: What else have we been talking about, huh, Sis?

SIS: Then when? I need to know. Tell me when.

FRED: I don't know yet. I've been too busy to think about it. I'll let ya know. You're not going to back out on our agreement are ya?

SIS: *What* is the agreement, Fred? I know what I'm supposed to do.

But I don't know what you're going to do . . .

FRED: Sis, just trust me, huh?

SIS: I thought you cared about Johnny! . . . Fred, listen, you've made it. That joke of pa's names you his number one son. His heir. You can sell. You can move . . .

FRED (*covering* SIS's *last line*): You mean someday . . . all this . . . will be mine? (*Hands* SIS *airlines tickets*) I've changed your tickets. You're leaving tomorrow morning at seven. First class. Courtesy of Eng's Chinatown Tour'n Travel . . .

SIS: Fred, just don't turn away . . .

FRED (*covering* SIS): Pa, I gotta askya something.

PA (*takes a letter out of his wallet and unfolds it*): I gib dis now, you teck it before gone porlay . . .

FRED: What . . .?

(JOHNNY *gets* PA's *glasses and hands them to* PA. PA *does not take the glasses but moves* JOHNNY *away with a wave.*)

PA (*looking at the letter*): Uhh . . . Chinee write down language . . . a lecker . . . It say . . . Uhhh . . .

(ROSS *looks over* PA's *shoulder.*)

FRED: Pa, listen . . .

ROSS (*reading over* PA's *shoulder*): It's about how to use farm equipment . . . animals . . . fertilizer . . .

FRED: Huh?

PA (*points at a spot in the letter*): "You momma anna poppa . . ."

ROSS: "Your parents" . . . Oh . . . "always have a plant or some animal in the house . . . uhh . . . some living thing." Umm. "Do not take easy money or steal . . . or cheat for money . . . If you do, you will be a thief . . . "

PA: Read later. (*Hands letter to Fred*) My pa gimme dat I leabing China. Okay? Okay, go now . . .

FRED (*puts the letter on the table*): Pa, I gotta askya something.

PA (*indicating letter*): Put in you pocket . . .

FRED: Pa . . .

PA: Late already. Going now. Come on, son. All togedders. Later . . . Spesul . . . banquets at Ruby Pagoda . . . My party . . .

FRED: I don't want to. I want you to tell Johnny . . .

JOHNNY: Why don't you tell me . . .

FRED: Because you don't do what I tell you!

JOHNNY: Who're you?

PA: Johnny, I talking Fred . . . (*Motions to his neck*)
(JOHNNY *gets* PA's *necktie and ties it on him.*)

FRED: I want you to tell Johnny not to do tours anymore.

JOHNNY: What'd you come back for. Whyn't you just stay out?

PA: Johnny! (*To* FRED) Dat all you wan'? What else?

FRED (*relieved, puts an airline ticket on the table*): That's all . . . I
got Johnny's plane ticket right here, and . . . (*Puts* SIS's *red envelope on top of the ticket*) Just tell'em.
        (PA *sits and* CHINA MAMA *and* JOHNNY *each put a shoe on* PA's
        feet.)

PA: You're hopin we're all gone when you're just come home now,
huh.

FRED: . . . Oh, I knew you'd be here. You haven't been able to
cough or bleed or take a crap . . .

MA (*makes a tentative move to go to the bathroom*): Oh, son . . .

FRED: Ma!

PA: Siddong. No singin. No bat'room. Nuttin . . .!

FRED: Well, pa, whaddaya think?

PA: Thing? What thing about?

FRED: How about Johnny, pa?

PA: Not much to ask, huh, son.

FRED: It's hard, pa . . .

PA (*motions* JOHNNY *to help him up*): Jacket.
        (JOHNNY *helps* PA *on with his jacket*.)

FRED: Well, how bout it, pa?

PA: Talk later! All go pour lay now . . . Stan'up, go now!

FRED: I can't.

PA: Donk argue me now!

FRED: Just tell Johnny not to do more tours and go take ma back east
with Sissy and Ross . . .

PA: Ma? Johnny? Da's stupid!

FRED (*overlapping* PA): They'll go if you tell'em, pa . . .

PA: Ah, ha. Ha. Come on, will you? Talk later. Ha. Ha.

FRED (*chopping* PA *off*): No.

JOHNNY: Why do ya want me outta here?

FRED: You and ma. Don't ya see what's happened here in the last ten years? Look at ma.

JOHNNY: Look at you!

PA: Johnny!

FRED: Yeah, look at me! What'd ya do, pa? Just stick me onto the first fifteen-year-old girl you met off the boat? You know I really, really think ma coulda been a singer . . .

PA: Ngaw gew nay . . . I tell you stan' up. Yes or no.

FRED: I can't.

PA: What you mean "can't"? Dis're mah house! You my son.

FRED: Tell ma and Johnny to go. I want everybody to hear it, then I'll go withya . . .

PA: Talking later, I tolling. Business first!

FRED: Tell'em, pa.

PA: You my son, yes or no?

JOHNNY (*overlapping* PA): The speech is for you! For you!

FRED: NO!

PA: What you mean "No"?

FRED: You gotta do somethin for me. Not for your son, but for me.

PA: Who you? You my son. Da's all. What else you ting you are. Huh? You telling me.

FRED: I don't care bout that, pa.

PA (*having never stopped*): Nutting else, da's what. You writing story, so what? Nobody read dat stuff.

FRED: I gave it up, pa.

PA (*having never stopped*): Meck funny dah Chinee. And (*indicating things shooting off in crazy directions*) Shoo! Shoo! Talking craze nevvah grown up! Now you're get up. No more probum . . .

FRED (*overlapping*): It used to be, before I'd come home to ya, after my last tour I used to write on napkins for a couple of hours. I'd be tired, but feeling all right. Made a few bucks, a few people laugh . . .

PA: What're you're talking laugh faw? Get up go now, I telling you.

FRED (*having never stopped, goes on*): Then this bald white guy came in and sat at the counter . . . And he was in my class in high school. And I don't want to talk to him. But he sees me and comes creeping down the counter at me . . . I hid my napkins and got involved with my noodles . . . ha . . . ha . . .

PA (*overlapping* FRED): Stop talking and do what I tolling you can't you? No arguments! Talk later . . .

FRED (*having never stopped, goes on*): "Didn't I go to high school with you?" he says . . . "Yeah, yeah," I say and he tells me he's married, pa, got kids, hates it, drives a truck for the *Examiner* and hates that and asks if I'm Chinese or Japanese . . . Ha. "Yeah, yeah," I say and want him to go away, and he asks whatever happened to the Chinese guy, Fred what'shisname, who was all kinds of student body officer and goin' to bust New York . . .?

MA: Didn't he mean you, Fred?

PA: Ma!

FRED (*having never stopped*): "Couldn't tellya, bud," I said. "Didn't he graduate with us?" "Couldn't tellya, bud," I said. Heh! Then the bastard sat down next to me and he sighed, pa. I looked straight ahead and there he was in the mirror behind the pies. People from the class before us were in the news all the time, he said. People after us were, you know . . . he looked at me over the lemon meringue and I was over the pound cake . . .

MA: It was nice of him to remember you after . . .

PA (*cutting* MA *off*): Ma! Me an' Fred!

FRED (*having never stopped*): And he said . . . "I wonder if anybody from our class will ever make it . . .?" And I wanted to say, "Me . . ." I wanted to, but I didn't. "Couldn't tell ya, bud," I said. Ha. Ha. Ha. I remember that guy cuz I was gonna surprise him. After you died. I was gonna go. Make it so big you'd only be remembered for having been my father. Nobody was gonna think of you without me.

PA: You never be famous . . . Jus' my son, da's all!

FRED: I don't wanta be famous. I'll never be famous, or write or act or nothin. All I want is for you to give me something I want and not to be ashamed of me for once. See me just once before you die, pa. Tell Johnny and ma to go with Sissy. Do it for me. Then I'll go withya to the parade. I'll stay in Chinatown . . .

PA (*slaps* FRED): You my son talking me like dat I asking you some-thing!

FRED: Pa . . .

PA: No maw argument. Go to porlay now . . .

FRED: No.

PA: You my son yes or no?

FRED: No.

PA: What're you say "no" for?

FRED: I mean no!

(PA *slaps* FRED, *who faces* PA *but doesn't raise himself from the chair.*)

VOICE: Hubba hubba! Hubba hubbas, folks!

(PA *looks around and sees all eyes on him.*)

PA: You my son! (*Slaps* FRED *again*)

FRED (*shouts above the voice*): No!

(PA *hits* FRED *again and again, shouting* "MY SON!" FRED *doesn't resist. He only shouts* "No!" *to each of* PA's *shouts. They shout and fall and clash around the kitchen as the voice of the parade exults . . .*)

VOICE (*wolf whistle*): Looka what're ya see ride on dat Caddies, Folks! Hubba hubba! From Chee Chee-cago dah Illing Noise! Da Missie Chinatown Bathing Suit! How bout a big hands, folks! Hubba Hubbas! An' here comes drawing da rears . . .

SIS: Stop it! Stop it!

(SIS *and* ROSS *try to catch* PA *and* FRED, *but can't.* PA *becomes as sluggish as he is vicious. He coughs and hacks. Keeps shouting and keeps up his attack*)

VOICE: Dah color gah da Cathay Pos' da 'merican Legions! Okay lady gennuhmans! Comes da dancy lahngs! Guardian . . .

(*"Lion Dance" drums and cymbals heard faintly outside.* PA *col-lapses.*)

MA: Wing!

FRED (*cold*): All right, get up!

(*All move toward* PA *but* FRED *stops them . . .*)

FRED: No! . . . Pa? (*Pats him. Moves the man's head*) Pa! Damn ya!

SIS: Is he . . .

FRED (*roughly dumps the body and jumps up*): He's a flop! Couldn't even make your stupid speech without hanging onto me couldya? You flop! "Mayor of Chinatown" Flop!

(FRED *drops to the floor and pulls* PA *roughly by the lapels, slaps the man's face and drops him.*)

SIS: Fred!

(ROSS *goes to the phone and calls an ambulance.* SIS *and* JOHNNY *pull* FRED *away from* PA *and kneel by the body.*)

SIS: Oh, pa!

FRED: I know that speech was for me. You don't know how bad I wanted you to make that speech, because I knew it was for me. I wouldn'ta understood a fucking word, but I'd have been so proud . . .! But you flopped! You miserable shit! You big mouth! Chi yeah dai pow! You frogdump!

MA: Oh, ah-jie! Your language!

SIS: Pa's dead, ma!

MA: Donk you think I know that?

FRED: Pa . . .

SIS: You've been waiting for pa to die. All right, he's dead now!

FRED: Shouldn't you be outside with your tourist husband? Downstairs! Outside! I got you outta here once; dammit get outta here now! If you were smart, Johnny . . .

JOHNNY: Don't you talk to me . . .

SIS (*cutting* FRED *off*): It's you! You're the one keeping Johnny here! He loves it here like you!

JOHNNY (*overlapping* SIS): It's me. Me . . .

VOICE (*ad lib over* JOHNNY, FRED, *and* SIS): Here're be come da good lucks, folks! Dah dancey lions obba China . . . whoo donk scare da kids! Ha. Ha. Ha. Now da lons dancing bow tree time. Good lucks! Goong Hay Fot Choy. One . . . Two . . . tree tahm . . . Listen! Hear dem balls? See doze lights? . . . Hear doze drum?

FRED: Get your shit and get outta my house. Go back to Mars! Go to Pluto! Move! (*Moves on* SIS *and* ROSS)

SIS: Johnny! Can't you see?

JOHNNY: I see you come from someplace I can't live, Sis . . .

FRED: Sis . . .

SIS: You're like some ugly new breed of rat who can't live without poison.

FRED: It's Warafin, Sis! Cyanide, Chinatown, take your pick and get out. Not a word outta you, Ross. You bought out, remember?

SIS: Johnny!

(*Bells, cymbals, drums in the background. Firecrackers lighten.*)

VOICE: Lady gennuhmans . . . dere it's are! Dah worl' famous, worl' longes' really Chinee Dragger inna worl' Ache hunner feet longs . . . dah boy runnings inna anna outta dragger keep it go dong dah strit once a year . . .

JOHNNY (*through the voice*): Lemme alone, Sis!

SIS: You're the poison, Fred!

FRED (*anger spent*): Pa . . .

SIS: Freddie, please . . . come . . .

ROSS: We've called the ambulance.

FRED: Oh, you did that . . . Well . . . I woulda liked to have packed him up into the Sierras and buried him by the railroad . . . I was savin that one for last . . .

JOHNNY: Aw, shuddup! Can't ya just shuddup!

FRED: No! This is my house now. Pa gave it to me. My ma. My China Mama. My Chinatown. My house! You all know that. If you're staying here man, you're mine!

(CHINA MAMA *takes a picture of* PA *off the wall and puts it by the red-painted coffee can full of sand. She lights a punk and sits in her chair. Lights fade down to* FRED, *who takes bills out of his pocket, removes what he has to to be dressed in solid white, puts on a white slightly oversized jacket, and appears to be a shrunken Charlie Chan, an image of death. He becomes the tourist guide.*)

FRED:

Well, folks, we been up and down these Chinatown hills,

Sucking up the sights faster'n the eye can see!

Yessir, so solly Cholly! Goong hay fot choy!

(*Drops spiel and goes for straight badmouth and has no control*)

Lemme take your picture! You fucking bok gwai low got a face carved out of rotten potato cured in dogshit, runover with a towtruck driven by Helen Keller in a puke fit on pills . . .

(FRED *reaches the end of language and does something loud in some kind of awful pissed off wounded animal language . . . He stops.*)

JOHNNY (*in offstage voice picks up for* FRED; *he's a friend to tourists*): You've whiffed strange grease and your drool tastes alien. Martian. And pulses and throbs alive and gummy on your tongue.

FRED: And you wanna spit!

JOHNNY (*offstage voice*): If everybody in the buildings ringing around Chinatown throwing echoes down . . .

FRED: Was to spit out their window all at once!

JOHNNY (*offstage voice*): People in Chinatown would be suddenly swimming in drool!

FRED (*recovers enough to finish*):

That happened back in the fifties

When spitting was the rage.

I'll tellya bout that someday.

I'll tellya bout the legendary rice runner.

The year of the Great Chinatown Rice Freeze.

The Chinatown caves and underground mushroom pastures.

But now you're hungry, folks.

And your tummy's shy of Chinatown chuck.

And empty and dark inside. A little homesick.

You don't feel comfortable about eating in a neighborhood that shows no cats.

The dogs here don't look healthy. And you seen garbage climb out of the trash wearing the clothes of old dead men.

And act like bums.

Makes you wonder what Chinamans eat, don't it?

I know the feeling . . .

BAD FEELING.

[*Curtain*]